# Stories of Positive Change in the Community College: Appreciative Inquiry in Action

Nancy E. Stetson

Company of Experts.net
Palm Springs, CA

For my daughters, Laurel and Nancy Lee, who – everyday – help make the world a better place. I am very proud of you both.

# CONTENTS

# Stories of Positive Change in the Community College:
## Appreciative Inquiry in Action

For information

Company of Experts, Inc.
777 E. Tahquitz Canyon Way, Suite 341
Palm Springs, CA 92262
www.companyofexperts.net
www.centerforappreciativeinquiry.net

ISBN 978-0-6152-3793-0

Printed in the United States of America

# FOREWORD

When Tom Gonzales, retired president of Front Range Community College in Colorado, was asked to describe Appreciative Inquiry (AI) in the community college, he said:

> What's remarkable about AI is its focus on what has worked successfully in the past and how it applies to the future. Academic institutions are about tradition. What better legacy for faculty and administrators than to share with a new generation an energetic new vision based on what has been successful? AI is about replicating those successes in changing times. I am constantly amazed at the energy that is created when you bring people together and they talk about the essence of their success. AI is not the latest feel-good fad; it's a proven methodology that draws upon the past to create a new positive organizational culture. AI is the antithesis of problem solving; AI is about appreciating people and processes that have worked and revitalizing the organization by emphasizing its many successes.

Gonzales quote from Stetson, N. E. & C. R. Miller (2004) *Appreciative Inquiry in the Community College: Early Stories of Success*, League for Innovation in the Community College, p. 38.

iii

# PREFACE

This book is designed to help community college leaders bring about positive change in the community college, change that will nourish student, employee and organizational learning, by plugging into the power of Appreciative Inquiry (AI). Whether you are a trustee, a chancellor, a president, a faculty member, a support staff member or student leader, you can use the power of Appreciative Inquiry (AI) to unleash the human energy in your community college to bring about positive and, sometimes, transformational change.

The first Chapter of this book gives the reader an overview of organizational learning, organization development, and AI. Chapter Two discusses an appreciative approach to organizational learning, including a brief history of AI, and some of the research and theory that generates its power. Chapters Three through Nine celebrate stories of positive change at more than 40 community colleges where, as Tom Gonzales said, leaders are using AI to create "new positive organizational cultures" by "appreciating people and processes that have worked and revitalizing the organization by emphasizing its many successes."

To be more specific, Chapter Three tells three stories about using AI for strategic planning: Berkeley City College, San Joaquin Delta College, and South Texas College. Chapter Four describes eight stories about using AI for teambuilding at Berkeley City College, Community College of Denver, Company of Experts.net, Corning Community College, Las Positas College, North Harris College, Oakland Community College, and Phoenix College. It also shares four stories of using AI for a combination of teambuilding and planning at Copper Mountain College, Mountain View College, Oakland Community College, and Ohlone College, and another five stories of using AI for planning at Amarillo College, Colorado Community College System and the Community College of Baltimore County.

Chapter Five focuses on two community college stories of AI in teaching and learning – the core mission of the community college – at Delta College and San Jacinto College, and another two stories at four-year colleges - Le Moyne College and Nazareth College. Chapter Six shares six stories about AI and human resource development at Lansing Community College, Centralia College, Asnuntuck Community College, Corning Community College, Delta College, and South Piedmont Community College. Chapter Seven describes how AI can be used in self study for accreditation, and tells three stories of community colleges that used AI for self study or a closely-related purpose: Community College of Denver, San Bernardino Valley College, and Clackamas Community College.

Chapter Eight highlights another nine stories about AI: assessing organizational strengths at Oakland Community College; celebrating successes at Rio Hondo College and St. Louis Community College: organizational culture at Bakersfield College, Houston Community College, and Southern State Community College; student engagement at Southside Virginia Community College; student recruitment and retention at Edison Community College; and teaching and learning at the Teaching for a Change Conference. Chapter Nine, the final chapter, shares some ideas about how AI is used or can be used every day, in a low-key way, at Santa Rosa Junior College and other community colleges.

AI also has been used in the community college for faculty development, departmental self study and program review, institutional renewal and conflict resolution, organizational culture, participatory governance, organizational assessment, celebrating successes, collaboration among diverse groups,

iv

strategic planning, and student orientation. These stories are documented in an earlier book, *Appreciative Inquiry in the Community College: Early Stories of Success*, fully cited in the Foreword of this book.

I hope this book will inspire community colleges that are already using AI to celebrate their successes and to be re-inspired toward more possibilities, and will encourage community colleges, K-12, and four-year colleges and universities that are just learning about AI to inquire into its potential and plug into its power. With almost 1,200 community colleges alone strategically located throughout the U.S. currently serving 11.6 million students, community colleges and other educational organizations can build on their considerable strengths and successes to bring about positive, sometimes transformational, change for students, employees, communities, and society at large. We all need all the help – and hope – we can get!

# ACKNOWLEDGEMENTS

I am deeply grateful to:

• David Cooperrider, Ron Fry, Suresh Srivasta and their colleagues at Case Western Reserve University in Cleveland, Ohio, who pioneered the early work in Appreciative Inquiry (AI), a radically different approach to organization development.

• Jane Magruder Watkins and Ralph Kelly, my primary face-to-face trainers in both foundations and advanced courses in AI. Also, Bernard Mohr, co-author with Jane of *Appreciative Inquiry: Change at the Speed of Imagination* – still one of my favorite books about AI.

• The legions of other people who continue to bring AI into my world through articles, books, conferences, listservs, websites and workshops.

• All of the contributors to this book, without whom there would be no stories to tell, most especially: Judy Walters, formerly at Berkeley City College and now at Diablo Valley College; Kathy Hart and Raul Rodriguez at San Joaquin Delta College; Juan Cruz and Shirley Reed at South Texas College; Leslie Prast and Connie Watson at Delta College; Ann Tate and Linda Watkins at San Jacinto College; Dennis O'Connor at Le Moyne College and the late Leodones Yballe at Nazareth College; Lynn Priddy at The Higher Learning Commission; Allen Butcher and Darlene Nold at the Community College of Denver; Kay Weiss at San Bernardino Valley College; and Rich Henry, Unified Field Associates.

• Charles R. Miller who, as my personal and professional partner for almost 14 years, helped me discover and explore the power of AI. Together, we brought the appreciative approach to positive change into a variety of organizations—primarily community colleges. While Charles and I are no longer partners, we each continue to grow individually from our association with AI, as well as continue to explore the power of AI in community colleges and other organizations.

• Charles, again, for helping me co-develop Company of Experts.net's four-day Appreciative Inquiry Facilitator Training (AIFT©) that was attended by more than 1,200 people from June 2003 to June 2008, in Canada, The Philippines, South Africa, Suriname and the United States, including 587 community college leaders.

• Kathy Becker and Jim Pulliam who currently own Company of Experts.net and the AIFT, for continuing to carry the torch for AI in the community college <http://www.centerforappreciativeinquiry.net>.

• American Association of Community Colleges and National Council for Staff, Program and Organizational Development for co-sponsoring the AIFT.

• Those AIFT Trainers, in addition to myself and Charles, who continue with the Company of Experts.net to train people to facilitate AI.

• The 165 two-year community colleges that, from June 2003 to June 2008, supported 587 community college leaders - chief executive officers and other administrators, faculty, support staff, students, and trustees - being able to participate in an AIFT. These colleges can call upon these and other AI Facilitators continuously being trained to help them plug into the power of AI.

Here are the names of those community colleges that have employees trained to facilitate AI, organized by Regional Associations/ Accrediting Commissions.

*Middle States and Others:*
Maryland – The Community College of Baltimore County, Frederick Community College and Montgomery College
New Jersey – Brookdale Community College and Raritan Valley Community College
New York – Broome Community College and Corning Community College
Pennsylvania – Community College of Philadelphia

*New England States:*
Connecticut – Asnuntuck Community College, Housatonic Community College and Tunxis Community College
Massachusetts – Middlesex Community College, Northern Essex Community College, Northshore Community College, Springfield Technical Community College and Quinsigamond Community College

*Northcentral States:*
Arizona – Cochise College, Glendale Community College, Maricopa County Community College District, Mesa Community College, Northland Pioneer College, Paradise Valley Community College, Phoenix College and Pima County Community College District
Arkansas – South Arkansas Community College
Colorado – Community College of Denver and Front Range Community College
Illinois – Morton College
Kansas – Barton County Community College, Coffeyville Community College and Johnson County Community College
Michigan – Delta College, Jackson Community College, Kirtland Community College, Lansing Community College, Montcalm Community College and Oakland Community College
Minnesota – Lake Superior College and Rochester Community and Technical College
Missouri – East Central College, Metropolitan Community Colleges, St. Louis Community College and State Fair Community College
New Mexico – Albuquerque TVI Community College
North Dakota – Bismarck State College and North Dakota State College of Science
Ohio – Edison State Community College, Northwest State Community College and Southern State Community College
Oklahoma – Oklahoma City Community College
Wisconsin – Blackhawk Technical College, Gateway Technical College, Milwaukee Area Technical College, Northeast Wisconsin Technical College, Waukesha County Technical College and Wisconsin Indianhead Technical College

*Northwest States:*
Nevada – Community College of Southern Nevada and Truckee Meadows Community College
Oregon – Central Oregon Community College, Chemeketa Community College, Clackamas Community College, Columbia Gorge Community College, Lane Community College, Linn-Benton Community College and Portland Community College

Washington – Bates Technical College, Cascadia Community College, Highline Community College, Olympic College, Seattle Central Community College, South Seattle Community College and Tacoma Community College

*Southern States:*

Florida – Broward Community College, Indian River Community College and Polk Community College

Kentucky – Kentucky Community and Technical College System

North Carolina – Asheville-Buncombe Technical Community College, Central Piedmont Community College, Guilford Technical Community College and South Piedmont Community College

Texas – Amarillo College, Brookhaven College, Cedar Valley College, Dallas County Community College District, Del Mar College, Eastfield College, El Centro College, El Paso Community College, Grayson County College, Houston Community College, Montgomery College, North Harris College, North Harris-Montgomery College District, Richland College, San Jacinto College South, South Texas College and Wharton County Junior College

Virginia – Blue Ridge Community College, Central Virginia Community College, Dabney S. Lancaster Community College, Danville Community College, Eastern Shore Community College, Germanna Community College, J. Sargeant Reynolds Community College, John Tyler Community College, Lord Fairfax Community College, Mountain Empire Community College, New River Community College, Northern Virginia Community College, Patrick Henry Community College, Paul D. Camp Community College, Piedmont Virginia Community College, Rappahannock Community College, Southside Virginia Community College, Southwest Virginia Community College, Thomas Nelson Community College, Tidewater Community College, Virginia Community College System, Virginia Highlands Community College, Virginia Western Community College and Wytheville Community College

*Western States and Others:*

California – Bakersfield College, Berkeley City College (formerly Vista Community College), Butte College, City College of San Francisco, Coastline Community College, College of Marin, College of San Mateo, College of the Desert, College of the Sequoias, Columbia College, Copper Mountain College, Cuyamaca College, Cypress College, Diablo Valley College, East Los Angeles College, Foothill College, Fullerton College, Glendale Community College, Grossmont College, Hartnell College, Las Positas College, Los Angeles City College, Los Rios Community College District, Merritt College, Mira Costa College, Moorpark College, Mt. San Antonio College, Ohlone College, Palomar College, Pasadena City College, Peralta Community College District, Rio Hondo College, Riverside Community College, Saddleback College, San Bernardino Valley College, San Diego Community College District, San Diego Miramar College, San Joaquin Delta College, San Jose-Evergreen Community College District, Santa Monica College, Santa Rosa Junior College, Southwestern College, South Orange County Community College District and Ventura College

# Chapter One

## ORGANIZATIONAL LEARNING

### Learning How to Learn

Leaders used to think of organizational change as a temporary condition, after which life would return to normal. However, as Bernard J. Mohr (2001), international consultant and writer, noted several years ago, ". . . we are increasingly confronted with a world in which change does not occur during a separate time period, after which we get back to business as usual. Rather, change is now the very water in which we swim" (p. 4). In other words, deep, rapid and often turbulent change is the *new normal* world in which we live and work.

In the new normal, how will community colleges best organize to get things done - the very purpose of an organization? In the industrial age, when life was more predictable and stable, command-and-control structures like bureaucracies and mechanistic ways of thinking, worked well for getting things done. Those community colleges that learned how to periodically scan the environment for opportunities and threats and *adapted* to them were more or less successful. However, in the new normal, adaptive learning likely won't be enough.

> *Adaptive learning* focuses on responding to and coping with environmental demands in an effort to make incremental improvements to existing services, products, and markets. It is similar to what Chris Argyris calls, "single loop learning," which focuses on solving current problems without questioning the framework that generated those problems . . . Successful organizations are ones that innovate rather than merely adapt; they "learn how to learn." Innovation, however, requires *generative learning*, which emphasizes continuous experimentation, systemic rather than fragmented thinking, and a willingness to think outside the accepted limitations of a problem. It goes beyond the framework that created current conditions that adaptive learning takes for granted (Barrett, 1995, pp. 36-37).

If community colleges are to remain healthy and vital institutions, they - like other postmodern organizations - must learn how to continuously learn. Furthermore, they must learn how to learn in a generative, not just adaptive, way. They must become more creative and innovative on an on-going, daily basis. How can community colleges develop their capacity to learn how to learn in a generative way?

### Learning How to Learn through Organization Development

Since the mid-1900s, Organization Development (OD) is one way that organizations have learned how to learn. What is OD? According to the late Richard Beckhard (1969), a pioneer in the field, it is an effort that is "(1) planned, (2) organization wide, and (3) managed from the top, to (4) increase organization effectiveness and health through (5) planned interventions in the organization's processes, using behavioral-science knowledge" (p. 9). Traditional OD is an "action research" model, one that helps the organization - often with the help of an external OD consultant - conduct research into what is working and what is not working in the organization, then take action based on the results. OD consultants typically interview or survey members of the organization to surface people's perceptions of what's going on in the organization, then summarize the data and feed it back to the decision makers who decide what to do to "fix" what's wrong or to "close the gap." The next step, often, is to do a force field analysis: to identify the forces that will support the proposed actions and those forces that will be barriers to those actions. Then, the decision makers come up with ways to eliminate or reduce the barriers to the desired change before trying to make the change. Traditional OD, then, is a deficit model for change: what's missing, where's the gap, what needs fixing. For 30 years, it was the predominant model for organizational change and development.

In the 1980s, a new approach to OD was developed and began to be practiced. Called Appreciative Inquiry, it also is an "action research" model; however, rather than focus on what is not working and fixing it, AI intentionally focuses on what's working and creating more of it. It focuses on possibilities rather than problems.

> Appreciative Inquiry (AI) is a powerful, strengths-based, and collaborative approach to facilitating organizational change and growth that is rapid, sustainable, and transformative . . . AI ignites this positive change because all humans . . . possess a 'rich reservoir' of cooperative potential, waiting to be unleashed. The essence of building cooperative capacity in human systems is to put the spotlight and questions on the good work, the best outcomes, and the most attractive aspects in that system. People engaged in this inquiry will naturally and quickly connect with their most positive beliefs about human groups and their potential to work, grow, dream, and celebrate together. They will naturally seek ways to move in directions that allow for more and more of that potential to be realized. The systems' capacity to cooperate around multiple initiatives will expand (Barrett & Fry, 2005, p. 101).

When it is at its best, AI uses a whole-system approach that involves all the stakeholders, or a cross section of the stakeholders, in generating the data about what's working exceptionally well and why, and then helps them learn how to create or generate more of it. AI also is based on grounded theory, that is, that the people in the system (i.e., the stakeholders) are the knowledge experts about their own system, rather than outside consultants (Cooperrider, et al, 2003, p. 39).

Bushe (November, 2007) offered a way of thinking about AI within the context of its being an action research model.

> . . . it invites members of a system to shift their mental maps and the prevailing discourse(s) in their system through a kind of inquiry that has no interest in validity, reliability, and generalizability – the kinds of things science values. Instead, in an effective AI the inquiry results in statements (provocative propositions) that are only generative in the system in which they are constructed, and their generative potential has as much or more to do with the level of engagement by all system members, and the quality of dialogue evoked, as with the actual 'findings' and provocative propositions themselves.

Classic and Emerging Organization Development Models

Most community college leaders are unschooled in the discipline of OD as a way of bringing about organizational or institutional change; usually, the closest brush they've had with it is some form of strategic planning, classically an adaptive learning and gap-based model. Now, just as some community college leaders are beginning to discover OD, the field itself is undergoing change. Seasoned OD practitioner, Robert Marshak (2005), summarized some of these changes.

According to Marshak, the old approaches to OD, i.e., classical OD, were based on an old paradigm or worldview, akin to deficit or gap-based strategic planning. In this worldview, the practice of OD was influenced by classical or Newtonian thought and philosophy, one in which organizations were viewed as machines. Social reality was viewed as an objective fact, there was a single reality, truth was transcendent and discoverable, and reality could be discovered using rational and analytic processes. OD practitioners collected and applied valid data using objective problem-solving methods that led to change. Change could be created, planned and managed, it was episodic and linear, and the emphasis was on changing behavior and what one does.

Marshak proposed that the new approaches to OD are based on a very different worldview, one in which organizational change is influenced by the new sciences and postmodern thought and philosophy. In this worldview, organizations are viewed as human or living systems, i.e., organisms. This worldview sees social reality as subjective and socially constructed through conversation and dialogue. Therefore, there are multiple realities, truth is immanent, i.e., it emerges from the situation; reality is negotiated and may involve power and political processes. Change is created through new social agreements that are arrived at by explicit or implicit negotiation (e.g., facilitated dialogue), is inherent, can be self-organizing, and is continuous and/or cyclical, with the emphasis on changing mindsets and how one thinks (p. 3).

Contributions to the new OD have come from a variety of disciplines, including psychology and neuroscience. Alan Deutschman (2005) described some of the new insights that help explain the power of language and mental models - both of which are key to understanding the power of AI. Deutschman makes three key points that are in alignment with the new approaches to OD and AI:

Real change isn't motivated by either crisis or fear. The best inspiration comes from leaders who can create compelling and positive visions of the future. Small, gradual changes rarely lead to transformation. Radical, sweeping changes are riskier but often more effective, because they quickly yield benefits visible to anyone. Narratives, not facts, guide our thinking. Data on declining market share or quality problems won't get employees to change what they do. Rather, appeals rooted in emotion are what best inspire people to alter course (p. 53).

Appreciative Inquiry: An Emerging Organization Development Model

Since the mid-1980s, AI has become both an increasingly popular approach to OD and an individual mindset or philosophy—a way of being, seeing and thinking; as previously stated, it is a shift from focusing on problems to focusing on possibilities. Here's how David Cooperrider, a professor of organizational behavior in the Weatherhead School of Management at Case Western Reserve University and the chief architect of AI, defines AI:

Ap-pre'ci-ate, v., 1. Valuing; the act of recognizing the best in people or the world around us; affirming past and present strengths, successes, and potentials; to perceive those things that give life (health, vitality, excellence) to living systems. 2. To increase in value; e.g., the economy has appreciated in value. Synonyms: value, prize, esteem, and honor. In-quire', v., 1. The act of exploration and discovery. 2. To ask questions; to be open to seeing new potentials and possibilities. Synonyms: discover, search, systematically explore, and study (Cooperrider & Whitney, 2005, p. 7).

(This approach) "is a powerful, strengths-based and collaborative approach to facilitating organizational change and growth that is rapid, sustainable, and transformative."

The assumption underlying AI is simple: every human (i.e., living or social) system has a core of strengths that is often hidden and/or underutilized - what is known as its *positive core*. AI helps people in the system search for and find the positive core. When the positive core is revealed and tapped into, it provides a sustainable source of positive energy that nourishes both personal and organizational change and, potentially, transformation.

AI is the ongoing, continuous study of what gives life to a human system when it is functioning at its best. A basic premise of AI is that, whatever people focus their attention on (i.e., study, inquire into), they will create more of it. Like using Google or other search engines on the Internet, what people look for determines what they find. So, instead of searching for problems or gaps and inadvertently creating more of them, people search for what is working well in the system (e.g., their own best practices) and then study them in order to learn how to create more successes.

AI proceeds with a study of an organization that is guided by three basic questions: What is X (the positive topic of inquiry), and when and where has X been at its best in this organization? What makes X possible? What are the possibilities that enhance or maximize the potential for X? The tangible result of an inquiry is a series of statements that describe where the organization wants to be, based on the high moments of where it has been. Because the statements are grounded in people's real experiences and history, people know how to repeat their successes.

AI also leads to *generative learning*; i.e., it "seeks to expand the organization's true potential" and to "challenge the status quo of the organization" (Cooperrider, et al, 2003, p. 112). Since the early to mid-1980s, AI has been used to facilitate extraordinary - sometimes transformational - changes in thousands of groups, organizations and communities in more than 100 countries around the world. Applications include organizational change, social issues, team building, individual development, and global and international applications (Sorensen, Yaeger & Bengtsson, 2003, p. 18). Many of these stories of success are posted at the international Appreciative Inquiry Commons website at <http://appreciativeinquiry.cwru.edu>, with more stories being added all the time. In a 20-year review of AI that was conducted in 2003, the reviewers concluded, "There is little doubt that Appreciative Inquiry has had a profound effect on the way OD is practiced" (p. 20).

In an interview with Cooperrider, the late management guru Peter Drucker said, "The task of organizational leadership is to create an alignment of strengths in ways that make a system's weaknesses irrelevant" (Cooperrider & Whitney, 2005, p. 2). AI is a way of creating an alignment of organizational strengths.

Learning How to Learn through Appreciative Inquiry

When first learning about AI, many people confuse it with positive thinking or focusing only on the positive aspects of organizational life. However, as Bushe (2007) eloquently explains, AI is not just about the positive; it is, more importantly, about the *generative*.

Generativity occurs when people collectively discover or create new things that they can use to positively alter their collective future. AI is generative in a number of ways. It is the quest for new ideas, images, theories and models that liberate our collective aspirations, alter the social construction of reality and, in the process, make available decisions and actions that weren't available or didn't occur to us before. When successful, AI generates spontaneous, unsupervised, individual, group and organizational action toward a better future (p. 1).

Note the words "spontaneous, unsupervised, individual, group and organizational action." The outcome of a successful inquiry is not an "action plan" in the common use of that term, with actions planned and assigned to people according to their job descriptions or their boxes on an organization chart. At its best, AI will result in inspired and improvised actions. At its best, AI will result in a change, or sometimes transformation, about how people think and, therefore, how they behave in the organization.

4

AI can be thought of as an appreciative approach to any organizational process, e.g., strategic planning, teambuilding, planning, teaching and learning, human resource development, self study for accreditation – virtually any process. For example, an appreciative approach to employee or student evaluation, or valuation as some AI practitioners call it, would focus on a person's past and current successes, helping the person uncover and build on strengths. It would not focus on the employee or student's weaknesses and try to "fix" them. In other words, the supervisor or teacher would be trying to help people, as Drucker suggested, to create an alignment of strengths, thereby making their weaknesses irrelevant.

## Five Generic Processes of AI

In organizations or communities, AI initially can be thought of as an ongoing cycle of five generic processes, which some practitioners call the 4 or 5-Ds (Mohr & Watkins, 2002, p. 5). However, as veteran AI consultant Jane Magruder Watkins has often pointed out, at AI conferences and on an international AI listserv <ailist@lists.business.utah.edu>, "AI is NOT the Model. Rather, it is a theory and philosophy that is far broader and richer than the steps that have evolved as a way of introducing AI into the planning processes of organizations and communities" (Watkins, 2007).

The five generic processes include: 1. Choosing the positive as the focus of inquiry (**Definition**); 2. Inquiring into exceptionally positive moments (**Discovery**); 3. Sharing the stories and identifying life-giving forces (**Discovery**, continued); 4. Creating shared images of a preferred future (**Dream**); and 5. Innovating and improvising ways to create that future (**Design**; and **Destiny** or **Delivery**) (Mohr & Watkins, 2002, p. 5).

### Choose the Positive as the Focus of Inquiry

In the first generic process, ideally a cross-section of the organization or community's stakeholders - sometimes called a Core Group – comes together and defines the overall focus of the Inquiry, i.e., what the organization wants to study in order to create excellence specific to the topic. Ideally, the focus of the Inquiry is focused on a strategic issue or issues. Because of a traditional problem-solving habit of mind, the Core Group sometimes finds it easier to identify an important or strategic gap, issue or problem - what the organization wants less of - and then reframe it into what the organization wants to study and create more of. The assumption is that whatever the organization focuses its attention on, it will create more of it. Therefore, topic choice is said to be *fateful*. The Core Group needs to mindfully and intentionally focus its attention on what it wants the larger system to study and learn from.

However, an appreciative approach to change can also start by identifying a process, structure, program, or service that is working exceptionally well and inquiring into the conditions that support its excellence or success. It can then transfer that learning to a new situation. In community development, this approach is called positive deviance.

*Positive deviance.* Community developers have learned that in every community there are certain individuals, known as *positive deviants*, whose special practices, strategies or behaviors enable them to find better solutions to prevalent community problems than their neighbors who have access to the same resources. Positive deviance is a culturally appropriate development approach that is tailored to the specific community in which it is used. One organization, Save the Children, used the concept in its community development work in Vietnam. The community developers, who had studied AI at Case Western, went into villages where children were undernourished. They looked for the healthiest child or children in the village and when they found the mother, they asked her what she did to help the child or children be healthy, i.e., conducted a mini-Inquiry. In one village, for instance, they discovered that the mother of the healthiest children fed them shellfish and greens from nearby rice paddies and also fed them three to four times daily, rather than the usual twice a day. The community developers then spread that story throughout the village so the other parents could learn from one family's story of success and help their children become better nourished (Berggren & Tuan, 1995). Within two years, 80 percent of the children participating in the project were no longer malnourished (Whitney & Trosten-Bloom, 2003, p. 86).

## Inquire into Exceptionally Positive Moments

In the second generic process, the focus is on inquiring into exceptionally positive moments of real and personal experiences of high-point moments in the system under study. This involves creating positive questions to explore the topic or topics of Inquiry and then using the questions to conduct interviews. The questions, as well as the positive topic, are also said to be *fateful*, i.e., the language of the questions will determine the direction the Inquiry takes (negative or positive) and the results of the Inquiry (negative or positive). Just asking the questions begins to bring about change in the human system, so the questions are deliberately *unconditionally* positive questions.

Participants are encouraged to pair up with someone they don't know well, or normally don't work with because a new relationship will result in creating or generating new knowledge. The interviews, ideally face to face, may end with each individual completing a Summary Sheet for the interview he or she just conducted. The Summary Sheet then can assist the person remember the highlights of the story or stories that will be shared and studied in the next phase of the Inquiry.

## Share the Stories and Identify Life-Giving Forces

After the face-to-face interviews, the pairs then usually form small groups, perhaps six to eight people. Again, people are encouraged to sit with people they do not know very well or don't normally work with. Group members take turns sharing the highlights of the stories their partners told them, everyone deeply listening to all of the stories. They then collaboratively identify the themes that were common and/or most exciting in the stories. These themes are often called the *life-giving forces*, i.e., conditions, factors and forces in the system that supported or nourished the exceptionally positive moments. Thematic analysis is "one of the most widely used qualitative research methods in the social sciences. It is employed to find commonalities, patterns, or trends in a group of subjects for the purpose of answering questions or forming theories about the group as a whole" (Thatchenkery & Metzker, 2006, p. 138). The small groups then "mine" the highlights of the stories and quotes to discover the positive core of the topic they are inquiring into.

Cooperrider and Whitney (2005) described the positive core:

The positive core of organizational life is one of the greatest and largely unrecognized resources in the field of change management today. We are clearly in our infancy when it comes to tools for working with the positive core, talking about it, and designing our systems in synergistic alignment with it. But one thing is evident and clear as we reflect on the most important things we have learned with AI: Human systems grow in the direction of what they persistently ask questions about, and this propensity is strongest and most sustainable when the means and ends of inquiry are positively correlated. The single most important action a group can take to liberate the human spirit and consciously construct a better future is to make the positive core the common and explicit property of all (p. 8-9).

*Mapping the positive core.* At this stage of an Inquiry, the small groups can brainstorm themes from the stories and create a list of the high-energy themes, threads and quotable quotes that were present in the stories. From the list, group members discuss and agree on perhaps three to five themes or threads that the stories or quotes of exceptionally positive moments had in common, and that also were the most promising and inspiring themes or threads on the topic of the inquiry. "Common" doesn't necessarily mean the same words; it does mean common in spirit. Contrary to some other change processes, the groups are encouraged not to vote for the best themes; instead they are encouraged to continue their generative dialogue until everyone agrees on and is energized by several themes, or generates new themes that emerge from the dialogue.

Each small group then can write its themes or threads on a clean sheet of flip chart paper and post it on the wall. They then can create a scatter-gram, a visual map of the positive core, in a variety of ways. One way is to give each individual several sticky dots and invite each person to place the dots, one dot per theme, on those two or three themes on the topic that are essential to them, that they personally most want to create more of. Then, as a large group, they can be invited to reflect upon the scatter-gram, to notice any emerging patterns. Again, they can be reminded that the dots are not votes but simply a way to display the energy of the group.

In the same (or different) small groups, they can discuss and agree, i.e., participate in a generative dialogue, on the positive core (i.e., life-giving forces, factors and conditions) that supports X at its best - one theme or thread, together with supporting ideas, that the group believes most gives life to X (i.e., most nourishes it). Participants are encouraged to: seek divergence, rather than convergence; synergy, rather than consensus; and higher ground, rather than common ground.

AI can be thought of as helping people uncover or discover the success stories of the *positive deviants* in the organization, those people who - regardless of the sometimes very challenging circumstances in which they find themselves - have experienced or created exceptionally positive moments of success around a particular topic. By sharing the stories, they discover the system's own best-practice stories and, by sharing them, infuse the system with stories that lead to more successes.

## Create Shared Images of a Preferred Future

In this generic process, small groups focus on creating shared images of a preferred future. According to Capra (2002), the ability to express a vision in a metaphor or image is an essential quality of leadership (p. 122). Creating shared images usually is a two-phase process: the groups may first create a visual image that best expresses the theme or themes they selected from the stories, then a word image. The phases also may be reversed - first words, then visual.

*Visual image.* With everyone participating, each small group can create a visual image - a drawing, song, skit, collage, dance, or anything else that expresses the theme and sub-themes the group experiences as the essence or positive core of the Inquiry topic. They can be invited to use whatever resources they can find, including creative materials sometimes provided at the session such as balloons, stickers, pipe cleaners, etc. Each group then can share its visual image with the large group and everyone can be invited to give appreciative feedback, telling the "performers" what they liked most about their visual image.

*Word image.* Then, in the same small groups, each group is invited to translate its visual image into a word image, called a Provocative Proposition (or Possibility Statement, Shared Vision or Dream Statement). After the group has developed a visual image, it is often quite easy for them to "morph" it into a word image of several sentences. If it is a large-group Inquiry over several days, e.g., an AI Summit (Ludema, et al, 2003), these statements may be several paragraphs long.

The purpose of the Provocative Proposition is to bridge the best of "what is" with the group's own speculation or intuition of "what might be." It is provocative to the extent that it stretches the realm of the status quo, challenges common assumptions or routines and helps suggest real possibilities that represent desired possibilities for the group. Criteria for a good Provocative Proposition include: Is it provocative? That is, does it stretch, challenge, or interrupt "habits"? Is it grounded? That is, are there examples, i.e., stories of success, in the system that illustrate the ideal as real possibility? Is it desired? That is, if it could be fully actualized, would the group want it? Do they want it as a preferred future? And, is it affirmative? That is, is it stated in bold and affirmative terms "as if" it were happening now, i.e., written in present tense language? (Ludema, et al, 2003, p. 183).

Here's an example of a Provocative Proposition that was drafted by a community college in California during a one-day AI Summit for strategic planning: "San Joaquin Delta College is a dynamic community of diverse individuals committed to student success. We embrace open communication, trust and respect in a collaborative learning environment." For details of this story, see Chapter Three.

The verbs are written in present tense, known as "as if" language, i.e., as if the vision were already happening because, in fact, it is - in those exceptionally positive moments that were discovered, or uncovered, during the paired interviews and ensuing dialogue. During the process of drafting the Provocative Proposition, groups are encouraged to think about what X would look like if it were happening *all* or *more* of the time, not just in exceptional moments. In other words, they are invited to imagine a future that is provocative, grounded, desired and affirmative - specific to the topic or topics of inquiry.

The small groups can then report out their Provocative Proposition to the larger Inquiry group. Listeners can be encouraged to give one-word "popcorn" responses to the words or phrases that give them energy. This can help everyone appreciate the power of language.

*Innovate and Improvise Ways to Create that Future*

Each small group can then focus on innovating and improvising ways to create the future they desire. Together, through dialogue, they can answer the question, "How are we going to make this happen?" They can be encouraged to be bold, creative and innovative and, as Bernard Mohr proposed at an international conference, make it *inevitable* that the dream will be realized. This often requires redesigning organizational structures and processes so that the Provocative Proposition can be realized.

First, each small group can be asked to create a number of Bold Ideas (or Strategic Intentions, Strategic Initiatives, or Pilot Projects) that the *group* is inspired to make happen and record them on flip chart paper or other technology. They can be invited to report out their Bold Ideas to the whole group. If desired, each individual can be given red, yellow and green index cards that they can hold up, as each of the Bold Ideas is reported out, to quickly indicate their opinion. As with a traffic light, red would indicate "stop," yellow would indicate "caution" and green would indicate "go." A quick conversation can take place among the individuals holding up yellow or green cards and the small group that originated those Bold Ideas.

Then, the individuals in each small group can be asked to make a statement of a commitment or action that they, as an *individual,* are inspired to take in service of the Provocative Proposition. They also can make offers or requests of others that will ensure realization of the Provocative Proposition or Bold Idea. These can be captured on signed Post It notes, posted to the appropriate Provocative Proposition or Propositions.

*Destiny.* For novices, the Destiny phase seems to be the most challenging process in the AI cycle to understand. At the closing plenary session of the 2004 international conference on Appreciative Inquiry in Miami, Florida, Barrett focused on the topic of Destiny and defined it as *ongoing and simultaneous* Discovery, Dream and Design - a learning/discovery paradigm.

Every human system already is an appreciative system, or it couldn't live as a system. There are places in every human system that are already spontaneously acting and reacting, and inventing as they go (i.e., improvising). Spontaneity, innovation and improvisation require an appreciative way of knowing. Every human system is already doing that or else, in some way, it will be in entropy or die, become a statue and freeze. Our task is to notice where appreciation already exists in organizations, groups and communities, and amplify it. That's Destiny! (Barrett, 2004).

Notice the word "notice." Appreciation is a mindset or perceptual lens. When an organization begins to incorporate an appreciative approach into the fabric of its culture, it becomes an Appreciative Learning Culture (Barrett, 1995), one in which people continue to learn, on an ongoing basis, from their successes and strengths. It becomes a culture in which employees and other stakeholders continuously improvise, creating and innovating new programs and services that grow out of the positive core of the organization.

## Transition

Chapter One gave an overview of organizational learning, organization development and a new approach to organization development called Appreciative Inquiry (AI). As Barrett & Fry attest, this approach "is a powerful, strengths-based and collaborative approach to facilitating organizational change and growth that is rapid, sustainable, and transformative." Chapter Two will further discuss this appreciative approach to organizational learning and some of the research and theory that fuels the power of AI.

## References for Chapter One

Barrett, F. J. (1995). Creating appreciative learning cultures. *Organizational dynamics*, 24(2), 36-50.

Barrett, F. J. (2004) *Living on the appreciative edge* [DVD]. United States: Appreciative Inquiry Consulting.

Barrett, F. J. & R. Fry. (2005). *Appreciative inquiry: A positive approach to building cooperative capacity.* Chagrin Falls, OH: Taos Institute Publications.

Beckhard, R. (1969). *Organization development: strategies and models.* Reading, MS: Addison-Wesley.

Berggren, G. & T. Tuan. (1995*). Evaluation of the save the children foundation (SCF) poverty alleviation/nutrition program (PANP).* Than Hoa Province, Vietnam: Save the Children Foundation.

Bushe, G. R. (2007). Appreciative inquiry is not (just) about the positive. *OD practitioner*, 29(4), 30-35.

Bushe, G. R. (2007). *Why appreciative inquiry is unlikely to generate research publications.* London: AI Practitioner, November, 8-11.

Capra, F. (2002). *The hidden connections: Integrating the biological, cognitive, and social dimensions of life into a science of sustainability.* New York: Doubleday.

Cooperrider, D. L., D. Whitney, & J. M. Stavros. (2003). *Appreciative inquiry handbook.* Bedford Heights, OH: Lakeshore.

Cooperrider, D. L. & D. Whitney. (2005). *Appreciative inquiry: A positive revolution in change.* San Francisco: Berrett-Koehler.

Deutschman, A. (2005). Change or die. *Fast Company*, 94, 53-60.

Ludema, J. D., D. Whitney, B. J. Mohr & T. J. Griffin. (2003). *The appreciative inquiry summit: A practitioner's guide for leading large-group change.* San Francisco: Berrett Koehler.

Marshak, R. J. (2005). Is there a new OD? *Seasonings*, 1(1), 1-5.

Mohr, B. J. & J. M. Watkins. (2002). *The essentials of appreciative inquiry: A roadmap for creating positive futures.* Waltham, MA: Pegasus Communications.

Sorensen, P. F., T. F. Yaeger & U. Bengtsson. (2003). The promise of appreciative inquiry: a 20-year review. *OD Practitioner*, 35(4), 15-21.

Thatchenkery, T. & C. Metzker. (2006). *Appreciative intelligence: Seeing the mighty oak in the acorn.* San Francisco: Berrett-Koehler.

Watkins, J. M. (2007). <ailist@lists.business.utah.edu>, May 22.

Whitney, D. & A. Trosten-Bloom. (2003). *The power of appreciative inquiry: A practical guide to positive change*. San Francisco: Berrett-Koehler.

# Chapter Two

## AN APPRECIATIVE APPROACH TO ORGANIZATIONAL LEARNING

### Appreciative Inquiry is Born

The birth of Appreciative Inquiry (AI) reportedly was unplanned and unintended. David Cooperrider, the primary architect of AI, was a doctoral student at Case Western Reserve University in the early 1980s who had an unusual attitude and curiosity. Suresh Srivastva, co-parent, was his adviser; he also had an unusual attitude and curiosity.

From 1980 to 1983, Cooperrider was involved in what became known as The Cleveland Clinic Foundation project. It was during this period, while practicing Organization Development (OD) at the Clinic in order to earn his doctorate, that he became interested in the positive characteristics of high performance organizations. Cooperrider completed his doctoral dissertation in 1986 in which he put forth an extensive and formal statement of the principles and supporting literature for the developing concept of AI. The dissertation was unpublished but was later revised for publication (Cooperrider, 2001).

The term, Appreciative Inquiry, was first introduced as a footnote in Cooperrider's report to the Cleveland Clinic in 1983. At first it was an approach to organizational change practiced by a small group at Case Western as noted in Chapter One; it has now become a worldwide phenomenon practiced in organization and community development in more than 100 countries. Cooperrider earned his Ph.D. and eventually became a professor of organizational behavior in the Weatherhead School of Management at Case Western.

Over the years, many practitioners have contributed to AI, now a recognized discipline in the field of organizational behavior and OD. Many colleges, universities and other organizations - including Company of Experts.net, a service provider of American Association of Community Colleges - offer courses and workshops in AI. Case Western offers a Master's degree in positive change and the famed NTL Institute offers a certificate in Appreciative Inquiry in collaboration with Case Western.

### Appreciative Inquiry Attracts Attention

In 1998, GTE, now Verizon Communications, received the American Society for Training and Development (ASTD) Excellence in Practice Award that put AI on the map in corporate use of AI. As the story goes, GTE had 67,000 employees and morale was at an all-time low - after layoffs of thousands of employees. Then, thousands of front-line employees were trained in the foundations of AI. They became a Positive Change Network and self-organized a wide range of initiatives, including: customer satisfaction surveys; studies of call center best practices; and appreciative processes for employee recruitment, orientation and retention.

In 2004, ASTD gave Cooperrider its prestigious Distinguished Contribution to Workplace Learning and Performance Award in recognition of his work in Appreciative Inquiry and the impact he had on the field of training and development, as well as for his pioneering thought leadership on building better organizations and communities.

# Research and Theory: Why AI Works

First explored by Cooperrider in his dissertation, the conceptual framework of AI and why it is a powerful approach to organizational change is well grounded in both research and theory. What follows is an exploration of some of the research and theory that continues to emerge.

## Theories of Individual Behavior

There are at least three theories about human behavior and change at the individual level. The theories focus on past, current and anticipatory realities. Freud and others constructed the theory that our individual behavior is determined by our *historical reality*, i.e., who we are is determined by our past. Lewin and Skinner put forth the theory that our individual behavior is influenced by our *current reality*, i.e., who we are is determined by our environment. Cooperrider and Srivastva put forward a new theory, the theory of *anticipatory reality*, that who we are is determined by who we imagine we can be (J. Watkins & B. Mohr, 2003, p. 50).

AI is based on the theory of anticipatory reality, i.e., we construct our *individual reality* through our expectations, hopes, dreams and beliefs about what will or won't happen in the future.

## Theories of Organizational Behavior

Srivastva and Fry (1992) developed a theory that addresses the nature of organizational behavior and change or organizational learning. This theory proposes that organizations find their point of highest vitality at the intersection of *continuity, novelty* and *transition*. Continuity is related to the Discovery phase of AI, i.e., that vital organizations know how to connect the threads of identity, purpose, values, wisdom and tradition that already support extraordinary performance. Novelty is related to the Dream phase of AI, i.e., vital organizations know how to innovate and create unexpected newness. Transition is related to the Design and Destiny or Delivery phases of AI, i.e., vital organizations know how to launch and manage planned and improvised change.

## A Paradigm Shift for Learning: from Problems to Possibilities

A paradigm can be defined as "...the generally accepted perspective of a particular discipline, theory or mindset at a given time" (Cooperrider, Whitney & Stavros, 2003). According to Cooperider, et al, there are two approaches to human systems change or learning: deficit-based, the classical paradigm approach; and strengths-based, a new paradigm approach.

The deficit-based or problem-solving approach works very well in changing non-human systems or solving mechanical or technical problems. Parts can be taken apart and fixed, then put back together; and change tends to be linear and predictable, i.e., have a cause-and-effect relationship.

The strengths-based, appreciative, or positive approach works very well in changing human systems or solving human systems problems (i.e., organizations and communities). The system is living and operates more like an organism, web or network. Whitney & Trosten-Bloom (2003) summarized the differences in the two approaches:

| *Deficit-based change* | *Positive change* |
|---|---|
| Intervention focus: Identified problem | Intervention focus: Affirmative topics |
| Participation: Selective inclusion of people | Participation: Whole system |
| Action research: | Action research: |
|     Diagnosis of the problem |     Discovery of positive core |
|     Causes and consequences |     Organization at its best |
|     Quantitative analysis |     Narrative analysis |
|     Profile of need |     Map of positive core |
|     Conducted by outsiders |     Conducted by members |
|     Deficit-based change | Dissemination: Widespread and creative sharing of best practices |
| Dissemination: Feedback to decision makers | Creative potential: Dreams of a better world and the organization's contributions |
| Creative potential: Brainstormed list of alternatives | Result: Design to realize dreams and human aspirations |
| Result: Best solution to resolve the problem | Capacity gained: Capacity for ongoing positive change (p. 17). |
| Capacity gained: Capacity to implement and measure the plan | |

*The Shift from Problems to Possibilities*

Author and professor of management K. L. Murrell (as cited in Cooperrider, Sorensen, Yaeger, and Whitney, 2001) described the case for generating organizational hope, rather than malaise and alienation, and organizational creativity rather than curativeness.

> The most central orientation that I believe exists in AI is in its dependence on a life-affirming position as opposed to a problem focused one. In this simple statement comes the spirit and soul of the AI activity. In this attention to the creative process, as opposed to the curative, lies the foundation of hope. Problem solving methodologies have swamped our discipline as they have almost all of the professions, at least in most of the industrialized world. The attention given to deficit and scarcity thinking is one of the most common patterns associated with organizational malaise and alienation. It is something we can change (p. 105).

When we focus the organization on what's not working (deficits, gaps, problems and what's missing), we unintentionally create negative images and flood the system with those images. The organization or human system can become depressed and have difficulty seeing a hopeful future.

When we focus the organization on what's working (strengths, successes, potentials and possibilities), we intentionally create positive images and flood the system with those images. The organization then finds positive energy for creating even more successes - sees a hopeful future of health, vitality and excellence. When individuals and groups focus on their strengths and successes, they are more creative and innovative. As proposed earlier, organizational creativity and innovation are important because organizations find their point of highest vitality at the intersection of continuity, novelty and transition.

*But, What <u>About</u> the "Problems"?*

At first glance, it can appear that AI allows, even encourages people to ignore problems or negative situations and to put on a "happy face" to mask important and real issues and problems. In actuality, however, AI doesn't ignore problems or issues; on the contrary, AI helps people deal with difficult or pervasive issues or problems by reframing them into the "something else" that they truly desire, i.e., whatever it is that they can imagine. AI helps people locate their past and present experiences of the "something else" they desire and *amplify* it.

In the problem-solving approach, the goal is to fill the gap or solve the problem in the situation. The questions people work with are: what's wrong and how do we fix it? In the appreciative approach, the goal is to realize the possibilities in the situation - with no boundaries on what those possibilities might be. The questions people work with are: What's working? What's possible? How do we make it happen?

A perhaps apocryphal story may serve to illustrate the difference in results. When NASA's space program leaders discovered that pens didn't work at zero gravity because ink wouldn't flow down to the writing surface, they used a traditional problem-solving approach. The "problem" was that pens wouldn't work at zero gravity. So, they hired Andersen Consulting to problem solve and, after 10 years and $12 M, Andersen created a pen that worked at zero gravity.

The Russian space group, discovering the same zero-gravity phenomenon, didn't "problem solve." They realized that it was possible to simply use pencils. As futurist Joel Barker (1986) said, "Problems that are impossible to solve with one paradigm may be easily solved with another one."

It may be worth noting that NASA, at its Goddard Space Flight Center in Greenbelt, MD, offers AI as one of five elements in its Leadership Alchemy Program. Other elements include action learning, emotional intelligence and relationship building, reading and reflection, and developing the presence of the leader.

More Research and Theory: Plugging into the Power

Additional theory and research that support AI come from four bodies of knowledge: the new sciences; power of image; power of words; and power of emotions. Each of these four prongs of the plug will be briefly explored.

*New Sciences*

For the layperson, Margaret Wheatley (1992), author and OD consultant, may best explain the influences of new sciences on organizational change models in an easily understandable way. She has been applying the lens of living systems theory to organizations for a number of years because she believes that organizations are living, self-organizing systems. She believes that these systems, i.e., organizations, have what all leaders crave: the capacity to respond continuously to change and the capacity to sustain themselves toward a simpler, more effective way to work.

Wheatley's central question is, how might we organize differently if we understood how *life* organizes? She draws on the science of chaos, evolutionary biology, quantum mechanics and field theory. From her work, she asks organizations to consider how they might organize if they were to:

Accept chaos as an essential process by which natural systems, including organizations renew and revitalize themselves; share information as the primary organizing force in any organization; develop the rich diversity of relationships that are all around us to energize our teams; and embrace vision as an invisible field that can enable us to recreate our workplaces, and our worlds (1992).

Notice that AI intentionally plugs into the power of the new sciences, including the concept of self-organizing systems. Dee Hock (1999) also believed in self-organizing systems, so much so that he literally "bet the bank" on it at VISA, thereby transforming the use of bank cards from one-bank-only to a self-organizing network of banks that honored all member bank cards.

*Power of Image*

A body of research relating to the power of image suggests that creating and holding positive images or visions of the future inspire positive actions in the present. These areas of research include: image theory; Placebo effect; Pygmalion effect; effects of positive and negative thinking; and affirmative capacity.

*Image theory.* Ken Boulding (1956) in his classic book, *The Image: Knowledge in Life and Society*, puts forth evidence that the images we hold of the future influence the decisions and actions we take in the present. Dutch sociologist Fred Polak (1973) also researched very large human systems, i.e., cultures, and determined that the rise and fall of a culture depends on whether or not the culture holds a positive or negative image or vision of its future.

*Placebo effect.* 30-60 percent of all patients show marked physiological and emotional improvement in symptoms of illnesses, simply by believing they are given an effective treatment, even when that treatment is just a sugar pill or some other inert substance. For certain illnesses, e.g., depression, there was an increase of about 7 percent in the placebo effect per decade from 1981 to 2000 (Psychology Today, 2004). Apparently the placebo activates the circuits in people's brains that relate to mood and the affective domain (Watkins & Mohr, 2003, p. 51). Placebos also play an important mind/body role in pain management. In 2007, the Public Affairs Office at Columbia University reported that scientists there have demonstrated "that the placebo effect caused the brains of test volunteers to release more of a natural painkiller," called opiods. The report was based on the pain management research of Tor Wager, professor of psychology.

*Pygmalion effect.* When teachers are told that certain children, randomly selected, are gifted, the children begin to exhibit superior performance that is likely caused by the teacher's behavior as influenced by expectations. The effects, positive and negative, become nearly permanent (Rosenthal and Jacobson, 1992). In other studies, successful managers were often ones who had a strong mentor as their first boss, someone whose image of them was positive and supportive.

*Effects of positive and negative thinking and talking.* Unhealthy people have a 1:1 ratio of good to bad self images. Healthy people have a 2:1 ratio of good to bad self images (Watkins & Mohr, 2003, p. 51). Teams of people exhibit a similar phenomenon. Highly functional teams exhibit a 5:1 ratio of positive comments to negative comments; functional teams a 3:1 ratio; mildly dysfunctional teams a 1.1 ratio; and dysfunctional teams a 1:3 ratio (Frederickson & Losada, 2005). However, this positive effect begins to dissipate at a ratio of approximately 11 or 12 positive comments to each negative comment.

*Affirmative capacity.* The brain has the capacity to work with an image, but not with a "not image." Successful athletes intentionally visualize successes and wins, not failures and losses.

In 1982 researchers at the University of Wisconsin conducted a study of the learning process by videotaping two bowling teams during several games. Later, members of each team studied a copy of the video of their efforts in order to improve their skills. But the copies were edited differently. One team received a video showing only the times when its members made mistakes; the other team's video included only the times when members performed well. After the bowlers studied the videos and acted upon what they had learned, what happened? Both teams did improve their game, but the team that studied its successes improved its score twice as much as the one that studied its mistakes (Mohr & Watkins, 2002, p. 2).

Notice that AI intentionally plugs into the power of image.

## Power of Words

AI is strongly based on the theory of social construction: we co-construct our *social realities* (in organizations, communities, societies, etc.) in collaboration and dialogue with others through our shared expectations, hopes, dreams and beliefs about what will or won't happen in the future - our anticipatory reality.

Berger and Luckman (1966) put forth the concept that human communication is the central process that creates, maintains and transforms realities, that reality is socially constructed. Social construction asserts that we use language and knowledge to create the world as we know and understand it (Watkins & Mohr, 2003, p. 11). Whitney and Trosten-Bloom (2003) captured the essence of social constructionism, the power of words, by proposing that words create worlds (p. 53). Notice that AI intentionally plugs into the power of words.

## Power of Emotions

According to the research of Fredrickson (2001), positive emotions: lead to increased creativity, intelligence and health; broaden attention and thinking; undo lingering negative emotions; fuel psychological resilience; build consequential personal resources; and seed human flourishing.

Positive emotions broaden the *momentary thought-action repertoire*, thereby creating openness to new ideas and new courses of action. Notice that AI intentionally plugs into the power of emotions.

## The Principles of AI

Theory, research and practice of AI have led to the development of eight principles of AI. These principles are derived from three generalized streams of thought: social constructionism, image theory and grounded theory. Social constructionism is the theory that human communication is the central process that creates, maintains and transforms realities (Berger and Luckman). Image theory is the theory that the images we hold of the future influence the decisions and actions we take in the present (Boulding, Polak). Grounded theory is the theory that participant observation is the best means of data gathering for those who are interested in understanding and describing living cultures (Glaser and Strauss). From these streams of thought, eight core principles of AI have emerged (Whitney and Trosten-Bloom, 2003).

1. The constructionist principle: words create worlds. Reality, as we know it, is a subjective vs. objective state. It is socially created, through language and conversations.

2. The simultaneity principle: inquiry creates change. Inquiry is an intervention. The moment we ask a question, we begin to create a change.

3. The poetic principle: we can choose what we study. Organizations, like open books, are endless sources of study and learning. What we choose to study makes a difference. It describes - even creates - the world as we know it.

4. The anticipatory principle: image inspires action. Human systems move in the direction of their images of the future. The more positive and hopeful the image of the future, the more positive the present-day action.

5. The positive principle: positive questions lead to positive change. Momentum for large-scale change requires large amounts of positive affect and social bonding. This momentum is best generated through positive questions that amplify the positive core.

6. The wholeness principle: wholeness brings out the best. Wholeness brings out the best in people and organizations. Bringing all stakeholders together in large group forums stimulates creativity and builds collective capacity.

7. The enactment principle: acting "as if" is self-fulfilling. To really make a change, we must "be the change we want to see." Positive change occurs when the process used to create the change is a living model of the ideal future.

8. The free choice principle: free choice liberates power. People perform better and are more committed when they have the freedom to choose how and what they contribute. Free choice stimulates organizational excellence and positive change (p. 54-55).

Transition

Chapter Two discussed Appreciative Inquiry (AI), an appreciative approach to organizational learning, including a brief history and some of the research and theory that supports AI. Chapters Three through Nine will describe ways in which community colleges are using AI to facilitate positive change. These stories primarily were drawn from the experiences of people who participated in a four-day Appreciative Inquiry Facilitator Training (AIFT©) from June 2003 to November 2007.

In Spring 2003, Company of Experts.net, under the leadership of co-owners Nancy Stetson and Charles Miller, developed and began offering the AIFT. A foundations course, it was designed primarily for community college and other educational leaders, including K-12 and four-year colleges and universities. However participants come from all domains and many different countries, including businesses and corporations, nonprofit organizations, churches, schools, governmental agencies and the military services.

Participants who wanted to become certified as AI Facilitators by Company of Experts.net needed to complete a practicum, i.e., facilitate an Appreciative Inquiry, and then submit a practicum report to demonstrate their ability to apply the knowledge, skills and abilities gained in the AIFT and during the facilitation of an Inquiry. A number of community college leaders submitted practicum reports, stories of positive change at their community colleges.

To illustrate the wide range of ways that AI can be used in community colleges, Chapters Three through Nine describe some of those stories drawn from practicum and other stories reported to Company of Experts.net or directly to the author. They are organized by organizational processes, e.g., strategic planning, teambuilding, planning, teaching and learning, human resource development, self study for accreditation and other processes.

# References for Chapter Two

Barker, J. (1986). *Discovering the future: The business of paradigms* [Videotape]. United States: StarThrower.

Berger, P. & T. Luckman (1966). *The social construction of reality.* New York: Anchor Books.

Boulding, K. (1956). *The image: Knowledge in life and society.* Ann Arbor: University of Michigan Press.

Cooperrider, D. (2001). *AI: The beginnings (Toward a methodology for understanding and enhancing organizational innovation).* Cleveland, OH: Crown Custom Publishing.

Cooperrider, D., P. Sorensen, T. Yaeger & D. Whitney (2001). *Appreciative inquiry: an emerging direction for organization development.* Champaign, IL: Stipes.

Cooperrider, D., D. Whitney & J. Stavros (2003). *Appreciative inquiry handbook.* Bedford Heights, OH: Lakeshore.

Fredrickson, B. L. (2001). "The role of positive emotions in positive psychology: The broaden-and-build theory of positive emotions." *American Psychologist*, 56, 218-226.

Frederickson, B. and M. F. Losada (2005). "Positive affect and the complex dynamics of human flourishing." *American Psychologist*, 60, 678-686.

Glaser, B.G. & A. L. Strauss (1967). *The discovery of grounded theory: Strategies for qualitative research.* Chicago: Aldine.

Hock, Dee (1999). *Birth of the chaordic age.* San Francisco: Berrett-Koehler.

Leaderships and the New Science, CRM Learning video.

Polak, F. (1973). *The image of the future* (abridged by E. Boulding from the Dutch Die Toekomst Is Verleden Tijd). San Francisco: Jossey-Bass.

*Psychology today* (2004). September/October.

Public Affairs Office, Columbia University (2007). *Columbia researchers demonstrate how Placebo effect works in the brain.* Retrieved August 29, 2007, from http://www.columbia.edu/cu/news/07/07/placeb.html

Rosenthal, R. & L. Jacobson (1992). *Pygmalion in the classroom.* New York: Irvington.

Srivastva, S. & R. Fry, editors (1992). *Executive and organizational continuity: Managing the paradox of stability and change.* San Francisco: Jossey-Bass.

Watkins, J. & B. Mohr (2003). *Appreciative inquiry for organization change: Theory, practice and application.* Workshop Resource Book compiled and printed by authors.

Wheatley, M. (1992). *Leadership and the new science*. San Francisco: Berrett-Koehler.

Whitney, D. & A. Trosten-Bloom (2003). *The power of appreciative inquiry: A practical guide to positive change*. San Francisco: Barrett-Koehler.

# Chapter Three

## STRATEGIC PLANNING

Community colleges are using Appreciative Inquiry (AI) both to develop strategic plans and, on a daily basis, continuously improvise or, as the long-time president of The George Washington University put it, continuously "troll for opportunities" (Trachtenberg, 2007). One approach they are using is the five generic processes of AI that were discussed in Chapter One, either as an ongoing, continuous cycle or as a one-time cycle for strategic change (Mohr & Watkins, 2002).

In this chapter, three community colleges tell their stories of success regarding their use of AI to develop strategic plans: Berkeley City College, formerly Vista Community College and San Joaquin Delta College, both in California; and South Texas College.

Berkeley City College, CA

Background of the College

> "The whole idea of AI is to make everyday conversations at the College focus on possibilities as a way of operating every day, rather than in exceptional moments or as the result of a Summit."

Berkeley City College (BCC) in downtown Berkeley, California, was founded in April 1974; Judy Walters was the president from 2004-07. She is now president of Diablo Valley College, also in California. BCC is the smallest of four community colleges in the Peralta Community College District, which covers six cities in the East Bay of northern California. Initially, the College was created as an outreach center - the entrepreneurial arm of Peralta. Its charge was to provide degree and certificate programs to the northern cities of Alameda County - Albany, Berkeley and Emeryville. Originally named the Berkeley Learning Pavilion, it quickly became the Peralta College for Non-Traditional Study (PCNS), a college without walls. Accreditation was granted to PCNS in 1981.

Several years later, PCNS became Vista Community College. It was housed in a leased administrative building in Berkeley and had at times rented classrooms in 200 locations throughout the service area. In 2006, a new permanent home was finally completed - a $67,325,000 building of 165,000 square feet—that officially opened its doors in August.

Vista Community College was renamed Berkeley City College (BCC) in summer 2006, to coincide with the College's move to its permanent location. Despite many last-minute surprises associated with the move, BCC's enrollment increased 14 percent from fall 2005 to fall 2006; by spring 2007, it was 18 percent higher than spring 2006 - over 5,000 students. And, in summer 2007, its enrollment was 100 percent higher than it was in summer 2006.

In spring 2005, the College ranked fifth out of 109 community colleges in California in transfers to the University of California at Berkeley.

**BCC's doors open in August 2006**

Introduction to AI

Before becoming president of Vista Community College in July 2004, Walters had served as vice chancellor for educational services for the Peralta Community College District. While vice chancellor, she had become interested in AI after attending a five-day academic leadership institute sponsored by UC Berkeley Extension in June 2002. The institute was an Appreciative Inquiry into the topic of *Leading Positive Change in the New Millennium* that drew approximately 40 leaders from two and four-year colleges across the nation.

In December 2003, Walters participated in part of an Appreciative Inquiry Facilitator Training (AIFT©) but was called away on business. Not to be deterred, she participated in part of another AIFT in February 2004 and – again - she was called away. Finally, just days after she was appointed president of Vista Community College, she decided that she and four other Vista leaders would participate in an AIFT in San Diego in July 2004.

**Judy Walters gives a
"thumbs up" to
Appreciative Inquiry**

The five leaders who participated in the training became known as the AI-5, a team that became responsible for introducing AI to the administrators at Vista. The group consisted of the president, the vice president of instruction, the dean of students, the Academic Senate president and the Classified Senate president. In September 2004, using the five generic processes described in Chapter One, they co-facilitated their first Inquiry; the positive topic was Maximum Inclusion.

Then, knowing that Vista would soon be moving into its first permanent facility, the AI-5 planned and facilitated a College-wide AI Summit (Ludema, et al) in October 2004 to help prepare for the transition. They wanted Vista to take the best of its past and present - its strengths, successes and values - to BCC. To discover Vista's positive core, the team selected the positive topic of Imagine Vista at its Best.

The Summit

**Administrators, faculty, staff and students engage in
dialogue to imagine and create the College's
preferred future**

At the October Summit, 72 people came together off site to engage in generative dialogue about the College's future: four administrators, 36 faculty members - both permanent and adjunct - 28 support staff and three students. For context, the dean of instruction first presented an overview of the College's student demographics. The participants paired up and used a modified version of the generic Interview Guide below to interview each other.

1. BEST EXPERIENCE: Tell me a story about the best times that you have had with your organization. Looking at your entire experience, recall a time when you felt most alive, most involved, or most excited about your involvement. What made it an exciting experience? Who was involved? Describe the event in detail.

2. VALUES: Let's talk for a moment about some things you value deeply; specifically, the things you value about yourself, about the nature of your work; and about this organization.

A. Without being humble, what do you value most about yourself - as a person and as a member of this organization?

B. When you are feeling best about work, what about the task itself do you value?

C. What do you value about the organization?

D. What is the single most important thing that your organization has contributed to your life? To the world?

3. CORE VALUE: What do you experience as the core value of your organization? Give some examples of how you experience those values.

4. THREE WISHES: What three wishes would you make to heighten the vitality and health of this organization? (Watkins & Mohr, p. 99)

After the interviews, they shared their own personal stories about the best of Vista Community College, including what they experienced as its *core value*. Then, in nine table-groups of eight people each, participants shared the stories they had heard from their partners. Each table group then brainstormed the common themes they had heard. From those themes, the table groups developed Provocative Propositions, or shared visions, about the college's preferred future and a number of Strategic Initiatives for realizing those shared visions.

Outcomes of the Summit

According to Walters, there were a large number of outcomes from the Summit and on-going dialogue. These included planning outcomes, organizational culture outcomes, shared governance outcomes, a name change and many inspired actions at the program level. Follow-up sessions were held in January and April of 2005 during which the College community came together to refine the drafts of the new Mission and Vision Statements. The participants also expanded upon the College's core values identified at the Summit, resulting in a Statement of Values.

*Planning Outcomes*

Planning outcomes included:
• A new Mission Statement: "Vista Community College's mission is to promote student success, to provide our diverse community with educational opportunities, and to transform lives."
• A new Vision Statement: "Vista Community College is a premier, diverse, student-centered learning community, dedicated to academic excellence, collaboration, innovation, and transformation. Vista Illuminates!"

• A Statement of Values.

The following Statement of Values was created:

1. Academic Excellence and Student Learning. We value our students' varied educational and experiential backgrounds and learning styles as well as educational objectives.

2. Multiculturalism and Diversity. We value diversity, which fosters appreciation of others, depth of understanding, insight, empathy, innovation, and creativity – characteristics our institution seeks in its students, faculty, and staff.

3. Preparing Students for Citizenship in a Diverse and Complex Changing Global Society. We value the fact that students live and work in an increasingly complex society and world.

4. Quality and Collegial Workplace. We value the high quality that characterizes everything we do.

5. Innovation and Flexibility. We value innovation because it encourages our students to question the "typical" and expand their thinking in a flexible manner, enabling them to understand life's dynamic potential.

*Organizational Culture Outcomes*

Before the Summit and immediately after the AIFT in San Diego, the AI-5 spearheaded a Vista Pride Day in August 2004, during which everyone worked, for the first time in several years to remove broken furniture, contractors were hired to clean the windows and carpets and to put new blinds on the College's leased administrative building. A second Vista Pride Day was held the following August during which faculty and staff had an opportunity to connect with each other before the start of the semester. The president and other administrators served pizza, salad and drinks to the workers.

According to Walters, the overall culture of the College was already beginning to shift, from a somewhat negative culture (believing they would never have a permanent facility) to one in which people began to share stories of good things happening - in the duplicating room, in committee meetings and in the interactions people were having with each other. People also began to make and keep individual commitments and feel as though "things were getting done."

In July 2006, during the move to its new and permanent campus, the College's shifting culture was stressed to its maximum limits. While the move had been planned over a period of nine months and existing leases for facilities were already cancelled, there were construction delays and, additionally, the local fire department would not sanction the new building for occupancy. So, with only 30 minutes advance notice, the College community planned and moved an entire College on one day in mid-July - from its old location to a newly-leased location nearby.

The College community also had just suffered the death of their beloved vice president of instruction and was grieving. Under the leadership of an acting vice president and the assessment officer, the staff planned and began offering admissions, registration and financial aid services to students in the leased facility from mid-July to the end of the month. During this two-week period, President Walters negotiated with all participating partners: the general contractor, City of Berkeley, Peralta District and Peralta vendors, on a way to open the new campus building in time for the start of classes. Administration set up a fire-watch and security for the new facility in order to have a shared occupancy between the general contractor and the College/District.

On August 1, Vista, now known as Berkeley City College (BCC) moved the entire College again, from the leased facility to the permanent building. At that time, only the east side of the first floor of the permanent facility could be occupied, so staff set up temporary admissions, registration and financial aid services for students until the permanent student services areas were completed in February 2007. During this time, BCC was closed to student enrollment services for only three days. Then, during the rest of

August, other units of the College - the library, administrative team and faculty - moved into their offices, just in time for the start of classes.

During the constant change, Walters said it was primarily due to the open collaboration among all employees that the College was able to "improvise" a relatively smooth transition into the new building. At first, briefings were held twice daily, then daily, then several times a week, then weekly, moving eventually into a longer time span to keep staff informed of the myriad changes that were occurring to the building schedule. From mid-July forward, Solutions Summits occurred monthly, to work with faculty on classroom and laboratory design and utilization and operations in the new building.

According to Walters, BCC's growing appreciative culture allowed employees to continue focusing on what was working in a constantly changing environment. This organizational attitude or culture likely supported the significant 13 percent growth in student enrollment. The other three colleges in the District did not experience this type of significant growth.

*Shared Governance Outcomes*

After the October 2004 Summit, a shared governance leadership council was established; it was composed of leaders from the various constituent groups: Academic Senate, Classified Senate, Student Body president, public information officer, vice president of students, dean of students, vice president of instruction, dean of instruction, business manager and a faculty member from the College's facilities and planning committee. During 2005-06, the primary focus of the council was on the move to the new facility. The council met twice a month and began the process of realigning the College's committee structure with the initiatives that the College had undertaken.

*New Name Change*

A new name for the College, Berkeley City College, became effective June 1, 2006 and coincided with the move to a permanent facility. The College's name is now identified more closely with its physical location, as well as with the world class University of California at Berkeley to which a growing number of its students transfer. The Peralta Board's unanimous decision in support of the name change recommended by the president was the result of collaboration - 14 months of surveys, dialogue and work among the College community and the community at large.

*Inspired Actions at the Program Level*

At the January 2005 follow-up session to the Summit, the College community developed an Inspired Action Plan for actualizing its Statement of Core Values. Following is a summary of those planned actions, as well as results and outcomes for each Core Value.

*1. Academic Excellence and Student Learning*

• To use teaching and learning strategies that respond to the many different needs of Vista students
• To be responsive to students' needs for access, convenience, and different learning styles through our scheduling and delivery methods
*Handbooks.* The Program for Adult College Education (PACE) program coordinator developed and distributed faculty and student handbooks that described the program.
*Proposal Development Workshop.* The College held a proposal development workshop in which faculty and staff came together to develop proposals for funding a variety of projects. Proposals were developed for:

• A linked basic skills program in Math and English
• An Independent Festival of Digital Arts and the Milvia Street Arts and Literary Journal
• A Difficult Dialogues program in International Studies
• A classified staff development program in communication and customer service skills
• A counseling department mentoring program to link underserved high school students, Vista students, and UC Berkeley students
• Better student services for a cohort program between PACE and the English department that serves mostly working adults.

The workshop provided an opportunity for people to come together to dialogue and to create new partnerships. Without additional funding, a number of outcomes grew out of those dialogues: a lecture series on Globalization and Women in International Studies co-sponsored by Black Oak Books; The Milvia Street Arts and Literary Journal now being sold in commercial bookstores; a linked Basic Skills program in Math and English that became the Foundations Program - English, Math, ESL, and counseling departments working in collaboration; and a renewal of the Student Ambassadors program with a focus on outreach to local middle and high schools.

## 2. Multiculturalism and Diversity

• To provide an environment that supports diversity in learning and self-expression with a curriculum supportive of multiculturalism
• To hire faculty and staff who reflect the diversity of our communities and students
*Foundations Program.* A team of faculty from Math, English, and ESL redesigned the College's Basic Skills program into a Foundations Program as a cohort model. The team studied models that were working at other community colleges, including cohorts, increased tutoring, and a strong link to student services. The Foundation's Program was launched in spring 2007.
*Cultural Events.* The College hosted a number of cultural events from 2004-07 including Indigenous Peoples' Day, Ancestors' Day, Asian Heritage Month, Cinco de Mayo Day, Students Constitution Day, Watershed Poetry Festival, Dia de los Muertos Week, Remembering Katrina Week, International Women's History Day, and International Women's History Month.
*Student Ambassadors Program and Collaboration with UC Berkeley.* Student Services worked to improve educational access for underserved populations by conducting extensive outreach through Student Ambassadors. Undoubtedly, this work helped produce at least some of the increased enrollment. The UC Berkeley Starting Point mentor program paired students from UC Berkeley with students from Vista for services such as tutoring and transfer guidance. BCC already enjoys a high transfer rate to UC Berkeley; it remains a high agenda item.

## 3. Preparing Students for Citizenship in a Diverse and Complex Changing Global Society

• To prepare students with learning experiences that help them develop cultural and global perspectives and understanding
*Global Studies Program.* An associate in arts degree in global studies was developed and approved by the Chancellor's Office for California Community Colleges in July 2005. The program later received a grant for a "green" community partnership with the Berkeley Ecology Center. Student interns developed a plan for an Earth Week exhibit and film festival in Spring 2007 that used Berkeley Ecology Center resources.

A Global Studies Lecture Series was initiated in Fall 2006 on the topic of Globalization and Women. Each lecture featured a local expert in the subject area. The program planned a series on Pandemics, arranging for experts to come to BCC and speak on influenza, AIDS and Avian Flu. The lectures were open to the Berkeley City College community as well as the broader Berkeley, Albany and Emeryville communities.

*Curriculum Development and Other Changes.* The Spanish department developed two courses in film and literary criticism to serve the large population of Spanish speakers. A course in Asian American literature was added to courses in African American literature, world literature and Hispanic literature. An outreach developer was hired to plan and generate educational course offerings in the community in areas such as life-long learning, in-service training, continuing education, ESL and basic literacy, service learning and other untapped community needs.

BCC entered into a collaborative arrangement called N'STEPS in conjunction with Rubicon Programs Incorporated, a non-profit community-based organization, to train entry-level workers in biotechnology. In Fall 2006, 25 students enrolled in the program and their schedule included Scientific Instrumentation and Scientific Literature. In Spring 2007, 10 of those students participated in a biotechnology internship while the other 15 students continued in math and English classes to upgrade their skill levels and to prepare for an internship and eventual employment.

## 4. Quality and a Collegial Workplace

• To implement review and improvement processes that constantly improve quality
• To develop leadership skills and respectful, close ties among all employee groups, in order to continuously improve the institution

*Vista History Project.* The Vista History Project continued to grow. Participants combed through thousands of photographs of Vista's history for display at the Thirtieth Anniversary Birthday Bash that took place in October 2004.

*Holiday Party.* About 75 students, faculty, staff and administrators attended a Holiday party in December 2004 at the Jazzschool in Berkeley. This event strengthened the already strong relationships that were forged at the Summit held in the same venue. An Open House was held at Vista's Fall 2005 Professional Day. All offices were open during lunch hour to provide information to all part-timers and newcomers about the function of each office. The offices of instruction and student services hosted guided tours.

*Leadership Development.* In Fall 2005, the president sponsored the attendance of five BCC leaders at the Dale Tillery Leadership Institute at UC Berkeley; leaders included the president, vice president of instruction, vice president of student services, Academic Senate president and Classified Senate vice president. Not only did it allow for training of a relatively new leadership team, it also allowed the team to spend four uninterrupted days together to develop a Student Equity Plan. In 2006-07, the president supported a faculty member and a classified staff member's participation in Association of California Community College Administrators' yearlong internship program.

## 5. Commitment to Innovation and Flexibility

• To celebrate the maverick attitude, which challenges conventional ways of viewing life
• To value innovation because it encourages our students to question the "typical" and expand their thinking in a flexible manner that allows them to understand life's dynamic potential

*Facility Plans.* Berkeley City College has a new six-story, 165,000 square-foot building. It was designed as a LEED green building, housing all services under one roof and was built to accommodate 7,500 students. Centered on a core atrium, the faculty, administrative offices and services are located on one side of the building, with classrooms and an auditorium on the other side. It is an open, light and airy environment, allowing people to function in new ways. In urban downtown Berkeley, natural light comes into the building from a huge atrium skylight. Also, all of the walls facing the atrium are glass, allowing natural light to filter down inside the building on all six floors.

The facility creates an environment within which individuals and groups are inspired to meet, talk, innovate and create. Groups of faculty, staff and students continued meeting after the October 2004 Summit to fine-tune departmental plans for the building. From the beginning, innovation and flexibility were the watchwords for the facility. The people involved in the design created spaces that could be used by more than one department and that could meet the pedagogical needs of the programs that already existed, and that could be easily reconfigured to meet future needs. Abundant and welcoming gathering spaces were built in the new facility to nurture the College's vision of being an ongoing learning community.

The College also held numerous sessions on how it would be "doing business" in the facility and what flexibilities would be required as people began operating in the new environment. Employees also created an All Employee Handbook that made it easier for new employees to become oriented to how BCC does business, as well as serve as a reference for veteran employees.

## Celebrating Stories of Success

The College celebrated its successes in many ways. One of these ways was through two internal publications that were printed and widely distributed to all employees: *BCC Today* and *The Messenger*.

*BCC Today*, published by the College's marketing and community relations office bi-monthly, featured in-depth stories of faculty, classified staff and students. It also featured a column written by Walters called Success Stories. Walters described the column: "These are stories of ordinary people doing extraordinary things. This is what comes to mind when we acknowledge the interesting projects and activities in which Vista people are involved and that need to be shared with everyone."

*The Messenger* was published semi-monthly, also by BCC's marketing and community relations office and featured news of interest to employees.

## Sustaining the Shift from Problems to Possibilities

The appreciative approach to organizational change and development permeated many daily activities at BCC. For instance, in shared governance meetings, when "problems" came up for "solving," leaders made a conscious effort to reframe them for generative dialogue by asking: What do we want to create more of in relation to this topic? When have we experienced success in relation to this topic? What can we learn from our best experiences?

Walters said, "The whole idea of AI is to make everyday conversations at the College focus on possibilities as a way of operating every day, rather than in exceptional moments or as the result of a Summit. I truly believe that BCC's strengths are its people, their creativity and innovation; from that positive core, we will continue to serve our students into a long and positive future."

In 2007, Walters left BCC to become president of Diablo Valley College. Her appreciative leadership style likely will influence the culture at that College.

San Joaquin Delta College, CA

Background of the College

San Joaquin Delta College (Delta College) in Stockton, California, was founded as a private college in 1934; it became public one year later. With a seven-member elected board of trustees, the service district covers 2,400 square miles and parts of five counties. Formerly named Stockton College, Delta College provides excellent, affordable education to lifelong learners. It currently serves 20,000 diverse students, including a large Hispanic population, in five locations - the main campus at 5151 Pacific Avenue in Stockton and four off-campus sites: Foothills, Galt/Lodi, Lathrop/Manteca and Tracy. Delta College also offers one of the most robust on-line, Internet-based course offerings in the Western United States; the College currently offers over 300 classes on-line, with an enrollment of 10,000.

Introduction to AI

> "Appreciative Inquiry matters because: it emphasizes the positive; it puts the responsibility on individuals; it engages and empowers staff; it unleashes creativity and innovation; and it puts people in control of their own destiny. In short, it is a 'better way of doing business.'"

In 2002-03, the state of California and, therefore, all state-funded community colleges, faced a fiscal crisis. Delta College alone faced a $2 million deficit and a mid-year cut of $3 million. The crisis caused employee morale to plummet due to the major cuts and austerity measures that needed to be taken.

It was during this crisis that, on August 1, 2002, Raul Rodriguez came on board as Delta College's new president. He had recently read a monograph about Appreciative Inquiry (AI). Rodriguez holds a Ph.D. in psychology, so he was predisposed to explore the potential of AI as an approach to change at Delta. He thought that AI might help the College community create, in the midst of crisis, a more positive culture at the College.

As a way of introducing AI into the culture, Rodriguez invited a pair of AI consultants to facilitate a mini-Inquiry with Delta's managers on a topic that was important to them - the broken relationships and lack of trust that had occurred as a result of budget and personnel cuts. By conference call, the consultants worked with a small cross-section of the management team to help them identify the important topic of Inquiry (*Generic Process 1: Choose the positive as the focus of inquiry*). The group identified the topic as relationships that weren't working, which was quickly reframed to Relationships that Work! - what the administrative team wanted to create more of. Then, after the conference call, the same group helped modify the questions suggested by the generic Interview Guide, making them specific to their topic of Inquiry.

In August 2003, all of Delta College's managers, including Rodriguez, attended an all-day, off-campus session in which the consultants co-facilitated an Inquiry into the positive topic of Relationships That Work! Using the modified Interview Guide, they paired up and interviewed each other about the exceptionally positive moments they had experienced when relationships had worked or were working very well at Delta College (*Generic Process 2: Inquire into exceptionally positive moments*). Then they shared their partners' stories in small groups and, together, identified the life-giving forces from the stories—those forces, factors and conditions that supported relationships that worked (*Generic Process 3: Share the stories and identify life-giving forces*). From those life-giving forces, they selected those forces or themes that they thought were most important or exciting and used them to create shared images of a preferred future (*Generic Process 4: Create shared images of a preferred future*). Then they came up with ways to create that shared future (*Generic Process 5: Innovate and improvise ways to create that future*).

During Generic Process 4, the small groups created eight micro Provocative Propositions of what it would look like if relationships were working very well all or more of the time. Later, one volunteer from each of the eight small groups met to synthesize the micro visions into one macro Provocative Proposition for the management team as a whole: "We, the Delta College Management team, serve students in an environment that fosters trust, open communication, collaboration and creativity to ensure the success of all students."

After being introduced to AI, the managers responded positively to the approach and its outcomes, and expressed interest in using it for further organization development and change. Since the College's Strategic Plan was four years old, they agreed that they needed to develop a new one and they decided to use AI for strategic planning, rather than the traditional approach known as SWOT, a focus on strengths, weaknesses, opportunities and threats. They agreed to focus on strength, opportunities, aspirations and results or SOAR (Stavros, et al, 2003).

AI for Strategic Planning

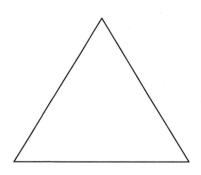

In September 2003, Rodriguez appointed an ad hoc Core Group of 15 people that represented a cross-section of the College: administrators, faculty, support staff and students. In October, the consultants met with 10 members of the Core Group to help them get clear on the topics of Inquiry. The first thing the Core Group did was decide to call itself the Delta Group because the "delta" symbol – a triangle - signifies "change" and because Delta also was part of the College's name. Members of the Core Group knew that they were about to embark upon a radically different approach to strategic planning and that they would be the leaders of the approach.

*Before the AI Summit*

The Delta Group decided that they wanted to involve as many stakeholders as possible in the strategic planning process so they decided to hold an AI Summit, a large-group change model. An AI Summit (Ludema, et al, 2003) typically involves a large group of people (30-3,000) who participate simultaneously in a three- to five-day Inquiry. However, the College only had one day in which everyone could come together in the same room at the same time. Therefore, with the help of the consultants, the Delta Group designed the strategic planning, or Inquiry process, so that some phases would happen both before and after the Summit.

The Delta Group identified the major topic of Inquiry as Imagine Delta College at Its Best! They also identified three sub-topics of Inquiry: (1) trust and communication; (2) service; and (3) creativity and innovation. At the October session, the group also modified the generic Interview Guide to make it specific to those three topics.

In preparation for the Summit scheduled for March 2004 that would involve a large cross-section, or microcosm, of employees and students, the Delta Group agreed to use the Interview Guide to interview as many people as possible in advance of the Summit, so that they could bring those voices into the room. Each Delta Group member agreed to interview at least 10 people and to invite those 10 people to interview others. A complete Interview Packet included the Interview Guide, as well as a Summary Sheet that would help interviewers capture the high-point stories and themes.

Delta College also decided to host an AIFT in February, prior to the one-day Summit, to begin building in-house capacity for sustaining an appreciative approach to change. Twenty-seven people from Delta College participated in the AIFT, including Rodriguez and members of the Delta Group. Others attending included the Academic Senate president, California Teachers Association (CTA) president, Classified Senate president and Student Body president. People who wished to attend the AIFT also were asked to interview 10 people prior to the March Summit, including some board of trustees and community members.

On the afternoon before the Summit, the Delta Group met again with the consultants who helped them draft a Statement of Values the group had distilled from the 175 Summary Sheets of interviews conducted to date. They also pulled out quotable quotes from people who had been interviewed about the best of Delta College and put the quotes on flip chart paper to be posted on the walls of the Summit room, thereby bringing those voices into the room.

*The AI Summit*

In March, 109 people came together in an off-campus location. Summit participants included President Rodriguez, the vice president for student services, faculty including the Academic Senate president and Union president, classified staff including the Classified Senate president and a student. [NOTE: it was difficult to involve more student leaders because the date selected for the Summit was in conflict with a previously-scheduled student field trip to Washington, DC].

**Raul Rodriguez, Delta College president, participates in an Appreciative Interview with Tena Carr, faculty member in Delta's Child Development Program**

At the Summit, the participants first validated a draft of the Statement of Values that had been crafted by the Delta Group. They then went through the five generic processes of AI and, as part of the cycle, validated 14 micro Provocative Propositions - visions of how they would like Delta College to be, based on the best of its past and present. One example: "Adjunct/part-time faculty are fully integrated into the College community with equal rights, responsibilities, and compensation." [NOTE: At the time of the Summit, Delta College was operating without an agreed-upon contract with faculty; they were actively engaged in collective bargaining].

All 14 Provocative Propositions were posted on the wall and people self-organized, i.e., voluntarily came together as small groups regardless of job category, around the Provocative Proposition that held the most energy for them. These groups then created multiple Strategic Initiatives (also known as Pilot Projects, Strategic Intentions or Pilot Projects) for realizing each of the micro Provocative Propositions that, again, were reported out and validated by the total group.

Then, one person volunteered from each of the small groups to work together, during a Summit break, to synthesize from the 14 micros a draft of a macro Provocative Proposition for the College as a whole. This resulted in a draft of a new Vision Statement for the College: "Delta College is a dynamic community of diverse individuals committed to student success. We embrace open communication, trust, and respect in a creative and collaborative learning environment."

**Small-group volunteers report out a draft of the College's new
Vision Statement**

*After the Summit*

After the Summit, the campus community was invited to come to the College's board room during several open sessions to interact with a number of items that were posted on the wall on flip chart paper: the draft Vision Statement, the micro Provocative Propositions and multiple Strategic Initiatives. Campus community members were invited to take a few sticky dots and place them on the items that held the most energy and excitement for them as individuals; they also were invited to volunteer to work on the Strategic Initiative or Initiatives of their choice.

From all of these processes, the Delta Group then finalized the College's new Vision and Mission Statements. After these were reviewed, revised and affirmed by the appropriate College governance groups, they were forwarded to the College's planning and budget committee - part of the College's formal governance structure.

The office of planning, research and regional education also created a website where progress was tracked on each of the Strategic Initiatives, including those initiatives that did not require additional funding.

*Hosting a Second Training*

In November 2004, Delta College hosted a second AIFT, in which another 15 people from Delta participated, so that the College could make AI a part of the regular way of doing business at Delta. In all, a total of 42 people at Delta participated in the two AIFTs hosted by the College.

## Integrating the Summit Outcomes into the Shared Governance Structure

In early December 2004, the Delta Group organized the Strategic Initiatives from the Summit into four major strategic goals in order to better track progress: open communication; employee development and training; increased student access and success; and increased financial resources.

Delta College then began integrating its strategic planning process with its budgeting process for 2005-06. For instance, by early March 2005, each unit of the College was invited to develop a plan and resources proposal (i.e., a proposed Strategic Initiative) that addressed one or more of four areas: (1) the new Vision Statement; (2) the new Mission Statement; (3) recommendations resulting from the College's program review process; and/or (4) one or more of the four major strategic goals. After training had been offered on how to use FileMaker software, administrative unit plans were then submitted on that program to the College's planning and budgeting committee.

For 2005-06, the College community submitted 341 proposals for funding, totaling $27 million. However, many proposals did not require funding; rather, they required a shift in how people focused their attention and energy. The President's Cabinet, in coordination with the budget office, then analyzed and approved 16 proposals and $500,000 in funding for those projects that required additional funds.

## Ten Strategic Initiatives and Their Impact

Kathy Hart, dean of planning, research and regional education, credits AI with jump-starting at least ten strategic changes at Delta College. Of those changes, the KUALI Financial System Development project was the largest and most expensive, and she believed would have the most impact on the College after full implementation. After the Summit, the College successfully developed a proposal for a grant that allowed it to join a consortium of universities that included Indiana, Cornell, Michigan State, Arizona State and Hawaii to become a full partner in the development of an "open source" financial system. Over time, the system would allow the College to save money that would otherwise have been spent on an off-the-shelf financial system. Hart believed that students would benefit from the savings because the College would be able to spend the significant savings on increased instructional offerings.

Three on-going initiatives directly benefited the instructional program: (1) a new-faculty academy that included a two-day new faculty orientation and monthly meetings during the first year of employment at Delta College; (2) an adjunct-faculty academy that included online orientation and modules; and (3) a faculty recruitment project involving internships for prospective community college faculty. A fourth project was a Fall 2005 flex day workshop for all College faculty to introduce and develop student learning outcomes for courses, a new requirement for continued accreditation by the Western Association of Schools and Colleges.

> **Using AI for strategic planning "made a HUGE difference in our budget process which was completely incoherent; now everything has to be proposed and justified as a project/program or an enhancement to one."**

An additional three projects directly benefited Delta's classified employees from proposals they submitted during the planning and budgeting process: (1) classified mini-grants for conference attendance; (2) annual funding for a classified retreat; and (3) funding for Classified Senate senators to attend a state-wide classified leadership institute.

According to Hart, another outcome of AI was the establishment of a College-wide professional development center. Formerly located in the library where there was limited access and called the faculty resource and development center, the professional development center now serves all employees: faculty - both full-time and adjunct; classified staff; and managers. The center has considerable state-of-the art technology and provides workshops for all employees on a variety of topics. The staff includes a full-time professional development instructor and a full-time professional development coordinator.

## Sustaining an Appreciative Approach to Change

The College shared qualitative stories of success throughout the College and celebrated those successes. It also developed quantitative institutional performance indicators of success for each of its four major strategic goals.

According to Hart, using AI for strategic planning "made a HUGE difference in our budget process which was completely incoherent; now everything has to be proposed and justified as a project/program or an enhancement to one. So instead of getting a request for more money for postage or supplies, these items become a part of something larger and it's easier to see why they need whatever it is."

President Rodriguez credited AI with bringing about a more collaborative approach to change at Delta College. Outcomes included: aggressive resource development; national and local partnerships; a successful bond issue and grants; and a reorganization of the College foundation. From the president's perspective, Appreciative Inquiry mattered because: it emphasizes the positive; it puts the responsibility on individuals; it engages and empowers staff; it unleashes creativity and innovation; and it puts people in control of their own destiny. In short, he said, it was a "better way of doing business."

Because the first round of using AI for strategic planning was so successful, San Joaquin Delta College held a second AI Summit for strategic planning in November 2006. People came together to celebrate Delta's past and current stories of success and discovered even more ways of appreciating, or growing, Delta's strengths, assets, capacities, capabilities, values, traditions, practices, and accomplishments.

Also, for several years, Delta was involved in a partnership with the Stockton Unified School District that used an appreciative approach to change. The purpose of the Stockton Education Partnership was to improve student success. Through AI and Delta's leadership, the schools began to experience increased student success.

## South Texas College, TX

### Background of the College

South Texas College (STC) is a multi-campus public community college system authorized to offer the bachelor of applied technology degree, located along the Texas-Mexico border just 90 minutes from the Gulf of Mexico in McAllen.

STC is the largest institution of higher education south of San Antonio, serving over 18,000 students throughout its two-county service district of Hidalgo and Starr Counties and their 700,000 residents.

STC offers a baccalaureate degree in applied technology and 90 associate degree and certificate options. The Southern Association of Colleges and Schools accredit the College as a level II baccalaureate degree-granting institution.

President Shirley Reed is the College's founding president. She joined the College in 1994 and took a simple, single-campus two-year institution of approximately 1,000 students and, by Fall 2006, turned it into a College district of three campuses and two centers enrolling over 18,000 students.

### Introduction to AI

In 2003, several STC administrators attended a League for Innovation in the Community College conference for community college leaders in which they learned about Appreciative Inquiry (AI). After the conference, they invited the conference presenters to come to STC in October of that year to introduce all of the administrators to AI by facilitating a one-day Inquiry on a topic of importance to them. A Core Group of administrators defined the important topic as Leading for Student Success.

After the Inquiry, the administrators expressed interest in learning more about AI and, in December, five of them participated in an AIFT in Houston. They were excited by the possibilities of the approach and went home to promote the use of AI as an approach to strategic planning; the administrators decided to try it out. In early February 2004, just prior to holding a one-day AI Summit for strategic planning, five more STC people - including the College president - attended another AIFT in Tucson.

### AI for Strategic Planning

The STC Planning and Development Council (PDC) is a body of faculty and staff committed to planning the College's future. The PDC believed that the strengths of the institution should serve as a guide and inspiration for even greater achievements as the College planned for the next five years. The PDC also believed that faculty and staff - those who worked diligently to fulfill the College's mission each and every day - should be the ones to create and share its vision of the future.

> "AI ignited the positive attitude and energy of 1,000 South Texas College faculty and staff, creating consensus and commitment toward the four Guiding Principles they helped create during Project Destiny."

AI proposes that every organization moves in the direction of what it chooses to study. STC chose to study its past and current strengths and successes - in the hopes of creating more successes in the future. The Inquiry process began with over 50 interviews in January 2004, using an Interview Guide modified by PDC, serving as the Core Group. The interviews sought to determine what inspired, motivated and compelled the faculty, staff and students of STC to achieve its many successes over its previous 10 years. Compelling stories of past and current successes were heard, strengths and successes that were woven into the fabric of STC's history. Those same strengths and successes also were woven into the fabric of STC's future through what people began calling Project Destiny.

Questions such as the following were asked repeatedly of all College personnel:

- What inspired 16,000 students to choose STC this semester?
- What strengths do we all share that make STC such a great place to be?
- What do we do best?
- What experiences and memories best answer these (and other AI) questions?

As story after story was told, interviewers began to identify a number of common themes. These themes appeared repeatedly in almost every moment, event and memorable achievement that had transpired since the College had begun to "improve the quality of life" of its students, families and communities. These themes were identified as the core strengths in which the College's achievements were rooted. The achievements born of these strengths were a reflection of the drives, hopes and motivations of the STC faculty and staff. They are what continued to draw the College community together to build, day by day, the STC legacy.

**An instructor, a staff member and a student are each interviewed for Project Destiny**

Juan Cruz, institutional research and effectiveness officer, then synthesized the themes and, in several meetings facilitated by in-house AI Facilitators, College employees discussed the interview data and developed descriptions of institutional strengths that would become the starting point for generative dialogue among faculty and staff at the College's AI Summit. Here are those descriptions.

*STC Provides a Small-Campus Culture*

STC provides the same caring, nurturing and familial environment that students have come to expect from a small-campus college.

STC is a warm and inviting place where faculty and staff know students - and each other - by name and always go that extra mile to make a difference in each other's lives.

STC is, most of all, a place where faculty and staff commit themselves each and every day to the care and welfare of every student's growth and success in higher education - and in life.

*STC Transforms the Quality of Life*

When STC enrolls a student, it transforms a family. The quality of life for an entire family has been improved when one student experiences success at STC.

The tenacity and persistence of our students, seeking to improve the lives of their families, should not be underestimated, nor should we forget the family that walks invisibly alongside every student when he or she comes onto our campuses.

We knowingly and willingly serve the family when we serve the student.

*STC Transforms the Classroom*

We continually achieve success for every student when our classrooms, and the learning experiences that occur within them, capture the imagination and transform the mind.

Students have continually risen to the challenges we place before them. They do so because we have empowered them with the willingness to succeed and self-actualize. And, we have empowered faculty with the ability and wherewithal to "make it happen."

To continue to experience such successes, this transformation of our classrooms must remain our highest priorities.

*STC Provides Greater Access and Equity*

Many residents cannot come to STC; we take STC to them.

For some with little to no transportation, the twenty miles to McAllen or Edinburg may as well be twenty *thousand* miles. STC is, after all, a *community* college.

STC is nothing if not available and equitably accessible to the communities it was created to serve. We, therefore, serve <u>wherever</u> we are needed.

*STC Has Community Support*

Our college is truly blessed with the support of its communities. Every day more and more residents are becoming aware of the positive and transformational impact we have upon their children and their future.

Faculty and staff are beginning to experience the same warmth, appreciation and encouragement from the community that faculty and staff have offered to the students each and every day.

Continuing to make such awareness possible outside the college requires that change continue to occur within. We must continue to acknowledge each other's contributions, sacrifices and successes, and interact with each other appreciatively and respectfully.

We must be the models for the social change we wish to see in the communities we serve.

*STC Values Its Faculty & Staff*

STC walks the talk when it comes to the importance of education.

Our most cherished and valued resource is our faculty and staff.

Our investment in their strengths and contributions, such as tuition reimbursement, sabbatical leave, and much more, has been, at the very least, a testimony to that sentiment.

Caring for our personnel, helping to grow their strengths and valuing their contributions has been, and remains, a primary interest of the college.

*STC Fosters the Courage to Succeed*

Of the many obstacles that bar our students from success, the two most difficult - that if removed, might very well open the floodgates to learning and academic achievement - have been the fear and self-doubt that reside in their own minds.

Second to teaching and learning, the college's highest priority is to create the sustaining and nurturing bonds that support and keep our students.

Every employee, instructional and non-instructional, is therefore encouraged and enabled to foster within each of them the courage to succeed.

*STC Strives to be the Best-In-Class*

STC is committed to being the best in class.

Innovation, creativity, self-drive and responsiveness are the hallmarks of our successes.

From the classroom to the boardroom and every room and office in between, STC is committed to being a recognized leader in higher education.

Nothing is more inspiring than a celebration of our successes and triumphs, and nothing is as effective for fostering more commitments to excellence than to shine the spotlight of praise upon those who have achieved it.

*STC is committed to being the best, and it shows.*

Continuing the Inquiry, the PDC, in collaboration with the College's professional development committee, invited all full time faculty and staff to participate in a daylong AI Summit at Dodge Arena in February 2004. STC rented the area's newest and largest large-events conference and entertainment center. The facility's indoor arena football field was filled with over 100 tables and 1,100 chairs.

Early in the morning of the Summit, the entire employed population of STC, custodian and counselor, file clerk and faculty, converged upon the Arena for a day of AI called Project Destiny. Almost 1,000 people showed up!

**People begin to arrive at the site of Project Destiny - The Dodge Arena**
**(Lower right, Shirley Reed, President)**

For the next eight hours, 25 AI Facilitators led participants through the 4-Ds or five generic processes of AI: Discovery, Dream, Design and Destiny. The day began with a brief welcome by President Reed, followed by a 30-minute video that showcased some of the highlights of the video-recorded interviews conducted in the weeks prior to the Summit. The interview segments were grouped into eight categories, one for each of the institutional strengths identified by the pre-Summit Core Group, so that the Summit participants would be able to hear and see for themselves how the many stories were woven into the College's institutional strengths. They would be able to see that seemingly random responses to interview questions focused on the same key institutional strengths, despite the fact that the people being interviewed had no contact with each other. In fact, the *positive core* of STC repeatedly emerged. The video concluded with a short explanation about AI, its benefits, purpose and strengths narrated by the faculty and staff who had participated in an AIFT and who had helped prepare the College community for the Summit.

The video was followed by an orientation to the day's events. Each of the 100 tables had been labeled with one of the eight institutional strengths. Staff and faculty were invited to self-organize at tables of approximately 10 people each, around the theme or strength of their choice. At each table, each participant received an Interview Guide that was specific to the table topic, as well as other information, including a Summary Sheet. Participants were invited to pair up with a tablemate and interview each other. After the interviews, participants shared each other's stories with others at their table and then followed the AI cycle through Dream, Design and Destiny.

Near the end of the day, a wireless microphone was passed from table to table as table speakers presented their group's Provocative Proposition or Dream Statement, creative Design work and inspired actions to fulfill STC's Destiny.

Flip chart papers from all of the tables were retrieved for continuing study by PDC. Many staff and faculty commented on how positive, inspiring, refreshing and "different" the experience was for them. Some people wanted to know more about AI.

*The Guiding Principles*

In July 2004, PDC held a retreat to develop the Guiding Principles for the future of South Texas College through a deep study of the knowledge created through Project Destiny. The most promising strengths embodied in the eight Dream Statements developed by the almost 1,000 faculty and staff were synthesized into four Guiding Principles. They were:

South Texas College:
- Fosters an environment for the students and community to achieve a better quality of life.
- Serves as the cornerstone for the economic vitality of South Texas.
- Is a premier learning-centered higher education institution where students and community success are paramount.
- Nurtures a culture where collaboration is valued and achievement is recognized.

**The Planning and Development Council meets to review the results of the February 17ᵗʰ Summit, Project Destiny**

From these four Guiding Principles, the divisions and departments of STC continually formulated specific, measurable goals for use in the development of institutional effectiveness and strategic plans for STC.

Project Destiny was a truly collaborative and inclusive strategic planning process in which all employees and other stakeholders had a voice in the future of South Texas College.

Juan Mejia, vice president for instructional services and chief academic officer for STC, had the following to say about the use of AI in his unit.

Bringing out the best in faculty requires focusing on what faculty are doing well and validating their direction. AI is non-threatening and showcases best practices and strategies that can be improved and replicated and therefore result in what we all are striving for . . . student success.

President Reed said, "AI ignited the positive attitude and energy of 1,000 South Texas College faculty and staff, creating consensus and commitment toward the four Guiding Principles they helped create during Project Destiny."

## Summary

Berkeley City College and San Joaquin Delta College in California, and South Texas College in Texas, generated positive energy for strategic change by using an appreciative, collaborative and inclusive approach to strategic planning. Many other community colleges also have plugged into the power of AI for strategic planning, including Tacoma Community College in Washington State and LaGuardia Community College in New York. These community colleges focused on past and current successes, strengths and opportunities to help liberate human energy for creating their desired futures.

## References for Chapter Three

Ludema, J., D. Whitney, B. Mohr & T. Griffin (2003). *The appreciative inquiry summit: a practitioner's guide for leading large-group change*. San Francisco: Berrett-Koehler.

Mohr, B. & J. Watkins (2002). *Essentials of appreciative inquiry*: Waltham, MA: Pegasus Communications, Inc.

Stavros, J., D. Cooperrider & L. Kelley (2003). *Strategic inquiry > appreciative intent: inspiration to SOAR, a new framework for strategic planning*. London: AI Practitioner, November.

Trachtenberg, S. (2007). *Keynote address*. Washington, DC: American Council on Education conference.

Watkins, J. & B. Mohr (2003). *Appreciative inquiry for organization change: theory, practice and application*. Workshop Resource Book.

# Chapter Four

## TEAMBUILDING AND PLANNING

Twelve community colleges, one consulting company and one statewide system reported using AI for teambuilding and planning: in Arizona, Phoenix College; In California, Berkeley City College, Company of Experts.net, Copper Mountain College, Las Positas College and Ohlone College; in Colorado, the Colorado Community College System and Community College of Denver; in Michigan, Oakland Community College - Auburn Hills Campus; in New York, Corning Community College; in Texas, Amarillo College, Mountain View College and North Harris College; and in Maryland, Community College of Baltimore County.

*Teambuilding*

### Berkeley City College, CA

> "I wanted us to see and hear each other away from the office, in a different setting, to help understand how people may approach an issue from a different perspective."

Judy Walters, former president and Jackie Shadko former vice president of instruction at Berkeley City College (formerly Vista College), in the Peralta Community College District in California, successfully co-facilitated a half-day Inquiry for Vista's six-member leadership team. The topic was Maximum Inclusion: Honoring Multiple Ways of Doing Things in the Service of Shared Vision. Walters hosted the Inquiry in her home. Of the six members of the team at that time, there were four women and two men: one African American woman, one Asian American woman, one Latino man, one Caucasian man and two Caucasian women.

Walters said, "This group is an excellent representation of our student demographics. Because we are a small college and every person has several jobs, we tend to work almost as independent contractors. As president, one of my jobs is to form a consortium of independent contractors. I wanted us to see and hear each other away from the office, in a different setting, to help understand how people may approach an issue from a different perspective. I wanted my team to see each other as an important part of our working group and I also wanted them to understand how we are all interconnected."

The team created a Provocative Proposition: "To create a climate of happiness and a culture of trust requires learning and working together through support and encouragement, respect, openness, sharing, communication, and valuing knowledge and skills with the common goal being to promote student learning and a changed society."

The leadership team came up with several Strategic Intentions and Individual Commitments. Walters, a relatively new president at the time, instituted a practice of awarding Certificates of Appreciation to College employees at the District's board meetings. She also regularly edited and published an in-house newsletter called *The Goodnews Newsletter* which was "about going through our daily work looking for the good stuff, telling others about it so that we can all appreciate that which nourishes us."

Shadko said that the newly energized management team was able to carry its focus into an all-college retreat. The success of the Inquiries launched a strategic planning initiative. For details of that story, see Chapter Three.

Judy Walters is now president of Diablo Valley College in California and Jackie Shadko is now president of the Oakland Community College, Orchard Ridge Campus in Michigan.

## Community College of Denver, CO

Barbara Wells was director of the Trio Scholars program at the Community College of Denver in Colorado. She facilitated an Appreciative Inquiry for teambuilding with her staff in which they developed a Provocative Proposition: "Trio Scholars is a group of students and professionals who are dedicated to the work of helping first generation students succeed through commitment, communication and compassion."

Each member of the staff then made a public Commitment to take at least one specific action to realize their Dream Statement. Wells said, "I had several staff come to my office to tell me how good the experience was and that they are very excited to get started. My personal best experience came from listening and hearing the common threads come from such a variety of stories. To be able to re-form the ideas into actionable plans was very satisfying for me and for everyone else."

## Company of Experts.net, CA

Kathy Becker and Jim Pulliam, co-owners of Company of Experts.net, co-facilitated an Inquiry for a community college in California to help strengthen the College's executive team and cabinet. Cabinet members were asked to identify their individual social styles ahead of time, using an inventory that assessed their behavioral pace (fast or slow) and priority (task or relationship) in relationships. Becker and Pulliam then developed a number of Interview Guides, one for each of the four social or relationship styles: analytical (slow and task-oriented), amiable (slow and relationship-oriented), driver (fast and task-oriented), expressive (fast and relationship-oriented) and for people's secondary styles. The Guides were then used in face-to-face paired Appreciative Interviews to help everyone appreciate and build on the strengths of each other's social styles (Merrill & Reid, 1999).

> "The best experience was observing participants 'get it'. 'Get it' means building from a positive perspective or visiting the past, evaluating the present and changing the future."

Using themes from the interview stories, the Cabinet members then developed a Provocative Proposition: "We commit to strengthening the Cabinet by trusting and being trustworthy, behaving as a professional team respectively while protecting one another as we take risks to meet X College's priorities."

One of the commitments agreed upon by all members was that they would listen more deeply to each other.

According to Becker and Pulliam, "The process worked . . . The best experience was observing participants 'get it'. 'Get it' means building from a positive perspective or visiting the past, evaluating the present and changing the future."

## Corning Community College, NY

Maarit Clay and Les Rosenbloom co-facilitated an Inquiry for the Student Services unit at Corning Community College. The team used AI to explore three topics: closer communication on the team; planning for an interim leader; and guiding the search for a permanent head. The Core Group indicated that the Student Services team was in transition and that the trust established in the AI process would be important.

46

> "During the Inquiry, one member of the team was inspired to volunteer to be the interim head of Student Development. After the Inquiry, the team was inspired to create a job description to be used in the search for the permanent head of Student Development. It included characteristics that were identified during the Appreciative Inquiry."

The session started with paired interviews, with this "best experience" question: "Tell me a story about a time when you felt most connected with the Student Services team in your role of working to help students. Looking at your entire experience with this team, recall a time when you felt most alive and most excited about your involvement. What made it an exciting experience? Who was involved? Describe the event in detail."

Thirteen people participated in the Inquiry, with one person pairing up with one of the facilitators for the interview. The team created a Provocative Proposition: "We are a unified student development team that integrates with other areas of CCC to provide a holistic college/life experience to promote and support the success of every student. We accomplish our work with a passion for student support and an over-arching integrity. We provide leadership in an integrated team environment where trust and respect are the integral base of our efforts. Our context is one of safety and support for our work so that we can add to the organizational context by contributing to an atmosphere of TRUE student development."

During the Inquiry, one member of the team was inspired to volunteer to be the interim head of student development. After the Inquiry, the team was inspired to create a job description to be used in the search for the permanent head of Student Development. It included characteristics that were identified during the Inquiry.

In a follow-up session, the Student Services team reported a variety of outcomes from the Inquiry: more interactions among participants; better communications; started communications flowing - before there was not a "place" to start; trust level was very low. Has improved markedly now; improved interactions. "Distances' precluded much interaction. Now we are really getting to know each other; never had a "retreat" to "bond" - AI acted as a retreat; lowered barriers of total strangers; Acting Dean's role is smoother as a result of sessions; AI allowed us to focus on a framework around the work to be done without leading the process; positive team building; brought separate agendas into the fold; commonalities emerged; everyone was heard regardless of "status"; explored the differences/values of what each department was responsible for and brought to the table and recognized how complementary things could be; and saw how each connected to the overall process of services to students-complementary wholeness.

> "... AI creates so much energy, the group fuels itself."

Additional outcomes included: everyone saw the big picture; small group process worked well (physical proximity); strengthened relationships - better understanding of the culture of Student Services; (Acting Dean said that it) strengthened my understanding of the vacant position - able to see other's values in the position; able to see what we all do and our commonalities; an expedient way to provide the President with group's recommendation; allowed us to feel better about our position and value to the college; empowering - allowing us to present ourselves to the rest of the college world; new people and department secretary are much more involved in the day-to-day functioning of the department; increased trust level; meetings have positive energy; process provides structure to allow others (new members) to participate in unit; and process increases power of the group process - allowing and supporting each other's epiphany.

Clay and Rosenbloom planned to continue AI when the new dean was in place. "We learned that the process allows the facilitators to step back, while providing some structure, because the AI creates so much energy the group fuels itself. In addition, the nature of the AI system allows those with diverging opinions the open space to express themselves in a comfortable, non-threatening environment. One personal best experience was seeing people working together so positively on the visual images. Also, the process of creating visualizations and writing Provocative Propositions manages to include all the participants at the table regardless of their communications preferences."

## Las Positas College, CA

Angella VenJohn was student interventions developer at Las Positas College (LPC) in California. While serving as interim dean of counseling, she facilitated an Appreciative Inquiry for the Student Services Coordinators Group -a dozen administrators (including the vice president of student services), their assistants and the counselors. The VP wanted the group to develop team cohesiveness and begin exploring the new ACCJC/WASC accreditation standards for student learning outcomes. The topic defined by the VP and VenJohn was Student Success and Learning. The first question in the Interview Guide was, "Tell me a story about your best experience at LPC in fostering student success and learning."

The group came up with a powerful Provocative Proposition: "We are a collaborative community of student services leaders who act in the spirit of honesty, integrity and loyalty and who value the individual and celebrate their success. We reach out and invite participation, promote personal change, and create growth opportunities so students can discover their personal potential, transform their lives and influence their world!"

> **"I learned the power of this process. Focusing on the positive creates a tremendous amount of energy and goodwill. It brought people together and created a synergy that was infectious. This diverse group realized for the first time that we were all here for the same reason . . . student success. And they now had a common language (AI) and experience they could build on."**

After a year of many personnel changes, the group found the sharing of their best experiences at LPC very moving and powerful. They were amazed that they shared many of the same feelings and thoughts about their experiences, even though they were in different departments.

As for her own learning, VenJohn said, "I learned the power of this process. Focusing on the positive creates a tremendous amount of energy and goodwill. It brought people together and created a synergy that was infectious. This diverse group realized for the first time that we were all here for the same reason . . . student success. And they now had a common language (AI) and experience they could build on."

VenJohn said that Appreciative Inquiry transformed her. "For me personally, I am truly moved by the AI philosophy. And I am trying to apply this strengths-based model to my everyday life. It makes so much sense to focus my energies on the positive, life-affirming situations in my life rather than the negative problems. In addition, I am considering going on for a doctoral degree. And previously I had thought I would get a degree in Educational Leadership or Educational Administration. Now after the AI training, I am considering Organization Development or Educational Psychology. Regardless of the field, what I must have included in my future course work is further Appreciative Inquiry education."

## North Harris College - Lone Star College System, TX

Melanie Hilburn, North Harris College, and Laurie Passmore, Lone Star College System – North Harris (formerly North Harris Montgomery Community College District), co-facilitated an Inquiry with the Center for Teaching and Learning staff at North Harris College in Houston, Texas. The

> **At the end of the session, "the group was laughing and people were looking forward to what they were going to accomplish."**

48

group identified the positive topic of A Team-Based Approach to Planning for the Future.

The nine-member group developed a Provocative Proposition: "We all play a part in shaping and carrying out the Learning Center Vision." The group also developed four Strategic Intentions for the Center: come to agreement on a common goal; value each other's roles; gather and share information; and strategize on how to implement the goal. Each of the members of the group also made an Individual Commitment. One example was to involve students in the Center's vision statement.

Passmore and Hilburn's wish for the inquiry was that the group would see "diminished tensions within the work group" and would develop "some level of cohesiveness." Apparently they got their wish! At the end of the session, "the group was laughing and people were looking forward to what they were going to accomplish." Also, in staff meetings that followed, there seemed to be more openness and willingness to work together.  As of January 2008, North Harris College changed its name to Lone Star College–North Harris.

### Oakland Community College, Auburn Hills Campus, MI

> **"I use the principles of AI on a daily basis by valuing what is best with my leadership team members."**

Sharon Blackman, former president of the Auburn Hills Campus of Oakland Community College in Michigan, became president of Brookhaven College in Dallas, Texas. Blackman participated in the first offering of the Appreciative Inquiry Facilitator Training (AIFT©), in June 2003.

Blackman facilitated a half-day Appreciative Inquiry teambuilding session for the 13 members of her leadership team at Auburn Hills. She began the session by facilitating a discussion about the difference between managing and leading. Then, team members began the Inquiry which resulted in a Provocative Proposition for how the team would work together during the upcoming year: "We have a vibrant campus community that fosters positive change, promotes cross-group inter-action and builds morale, using teamwork and communication while working toward common goals." Blackman had the Provocative Proposition printed and framed and distributed to each team member for them to place in their office as a reminder of what they as a group wanted as their preferred future.

After the session, Blackman reported, "The group has taken the 'team' concept seriously and work together to help the campus develop new initiatives or resolve campus issues. I have found President's staff meetings to be open where one is willing to speak up and offer a suggestion, as well as ask for assistance in attempting to resolve an issue. The team is relaxed with one another and acknowledges each other when something is done well."

In terms of follow-up, Blackman said, "I plan to conduct an assessment at the end of the academic year with the group in another retreat to determine how well we did in accomplishing our Proposition. I plan to use the AI tools to help us set our 'team' goals for the next year. I also meet with each team member on an individual basis each month and, during this meeting, we often address issues that work towards implementing the Proposition.

She also said, "I use the principles of AI on a daily basis by valuing what is best with my leadership team members. When we are faced with difficult tasks, the question is, what would we like to achieve and what are we doing now that is helping us to achieve our goal?"

### Phoenix College, AZ

Emily Weinacker, coordinator of employee and organizational learning for Maricopa Community Colleges, facilitated an Inquiry, an all-day retreat for the 16 members of a work unit at Phoenix College in Phoenix, Arizona.

According to Weinacker, the Office had divided and organized around "old timers" and "new timers." Coincidentally, the division happened to be along racial lines as well, i.e., most seasoned employees were white and most new employees were Hispanic. The administration allowed the office to close down for a day - a precedent - so that all staff could attend the retreat. Desired outcomes of the Inquiry were: increased teamwork and cohesiveness; a set of Possibility Statements or Values related to diverse teamwork; and a set of inspired action plans to achieve the Possibility Statements.

Prior to the retreat, Weinacker met with the director of work unit and outlined two options, a traditional approach or an appreciative approach to teambuilding. The director selected the appreciative approach. Emily then developed the format for the day and the appreciative questions.

> **"By the end of the day, there was still one person who was skeptical, but the energy level for everyone else was very high. Most people were saying: "I learned that everyone is having some of the same issues and that we are not all that different."**

Interview Guide - Teamwork

In today's diverse and ever-changing environment, teamwork is an essential ingredient for success. In high performance departments, teamwork fosters collaboration between diverse individuals and results in the department's being easy to do business with. Winning teamwork requires appreciation of differences, common goals, open communication, and full participation in planning and decision-making. Most people work best in a team environment where enthusiasm and team spirit are high, where ideas and information are shared, where team members work together to accomplish common goals, and where each team member is appreciated for the strengths and differences he/she brings to the team. It has been said that the results of teamwork are greater than the sum of the parts. The synergy that comes from winning teamwork adds value to team members, customers and the organization.

1. Imagine into the future . . . your department is one that exemplifies teamwork in a diverse environment . . . due to this, it benefits tremendously . . . it offers a special sensitivity to a diverse student base . . . What do you see and hear in this department? What is it like working in this department?

2. What are things you value deeply related to teamwork in a diverse environment?
Without being humble, what do you value most about your ability to work on a diverse team?
When you are feeling best about your work on our diverse team, what do you value about it?
What is it about our department's ability to be a diverse team that you value?

3. If you had three wishes for this department related to teamwork in our diverse environment what would they be?
(Interview questions adapted from *Encyclopedia of Positive Questions*)

At the retreat, Weinacker facilitated the group's development of three Possibility Statements focused on three shared values: respect, communication and appreciation. She facilitated a round robin Design process where each person rotated from table-topic to table-topic. A "champion" stayed with each of the three Possibility Statements to record Commitments, Offers and Requests, i.e., inspired action plans.

The champions recorded the Commitments, Offers and Requests generated at their tables. The champions also met the next day to outline their course of action, assemble the final propositions into "memory" form and decide what they would do with what Weinacker said were "beautiful Possibility drawings."

The three champions compiled all of the Commitments, Offers and Requests and worked towards organizing to get the job done. Weinacker worked with the champions to outline potential courses of action they could take. She also provided contact information so they could call her at anytime.

Weinacker said, "There were two points very early in the process - right after the welcome, before I was introduced and right after showing the video (i.e., Celebrate What's Right With the World) - where we could have slipped into 'problem solving' mode. I dealt with those interruptions in a positive manner using reflective listening and appreciative responses and steered them back to the process. By the end of the day, there was still one person who was skeptical, but the energy level for everyone else was very high. Most people were saying: 'I learned that everyone is having some of the same issues and that we are not all that different.'"

Weinacker left them with the idea that change was a process, not an event. She challenged them to follow through on their commitments and they would notice immediate change.

*Teambuilding and Planning*

Copper Mountain College, CA

"The session took place on a Friday and by Monday afternoon some of the Intentions had been accomplished or were started."

Sue Tsuda, coordinator of workforce development, described the "demonstrable results" of the Inquiry she facilitated with the staff (i.e., student workers and full and part-time (employees) of the Workforce Development/Transfer Empowerment Center at Copper Mountain College in California. "The session took place on a Friday and by Monday afternoon some of the Intentions had been accomplished or were started." The purpose of the Inquiry was to build one team from two different staffs and then collaboratively plan services for students.

The Center team members developed a Provocative Proposition based on their best experiences of the Center, their values and their wishes for the future. They also created 11 Strategic Intentions which were implemented and then celebrated at a follow-up meeting. Tsuda said, "I think my 'personal best' experience was the comment Carole Lasquade made about 'SOARing' rather than 'SWOTing' and the affirmative comments the team members made about the experience" (Stavros, 2003).

Mountain View College, TX

Charles Miller and Nancy Stetson, consultants, used an appreciative approach to teambuilding and planning at Mountain View College (MVC), one of the colleges in the Dallas County Community College District, in Texas. At the request of the president, Felix Zamorra, Miller and Stetson facilitated a 1-1/2 day

"In an incredibly short period of time, all kinds of creative and innovative ideas were generated!"

retreat for approximately 20 College leaders – faculty and administrators - in the spring.

The first day, a half day, a new research and planning officer, Jerry Scheerer, presented environmental scanning data that he had pulled together from three sources of internal data and three sources of external data. The research and planning officer – at the request of Stetson and Miller – focused on what was working well at the College, i.e., its Strengths and Opportunities in the external environment. (Stavros, 2003). He presented the data in very short powerpoint slides, backed up with a detailed data book. Each short presentation was followed by small-group brainstorms of internal Strengths and external

Opportunities generated by the data. Stetson said, "In an incredibly short period of time, all kinds of creative and innovative ideas were generated!"

The second day, with the earlier session as context, Miller and Stetson co-facilitated an Inquiry: Imagine Mountain View College at Its Best, for College leaders. The outcomes were drafts of a Vision Statement, Core Values and a Provocative Proposition regarding Working Relationships. The Vision Statement for the College, a macro Provocative Proposition, was "Mountain View College is a diverse and inclusive community of life-long learners committed to empowering people to transform their lives throughout their educational journey."

Stetson returned for a day in the fall. She gave an overview of AI to all employees in the morning, including the draft of the Vision Statement and Core Values. After lunch, employees spent two hours in a mini-Inquiry, focusing on the five core values that were developed in the spring: Mountain View College: Is Dedicated to Student Learning; Promotes Teamwork; Celebrates Diversity; Celebrates Student and Employee Success; and Values Contributions. People self-organized in tables around the core value they most wanted to bring to life. They paired up and interviewed each other with an Interview Guide that was specific to their chosen Core Value. Then they developed a micro Provocative Proposition for their Core Value and at least one Bold Idea for realizing their Provocative Proposition. For example, the Provocative Proposition for Celebrates Diversity was, "We, the people of MVC, are dedicated to the celebration of diversity, while actively embracing the education and integration of such into a network of cultural diversity." The small group agreed that they would organize a We the People Day, a celebration of their diversity that would include food, music and events.

Following the mini-Inquiry, Stetson facilitated another mini-Inquiry for the College leaders on Communications and Relationships. This session grew out of the spring session in which the same group had developed a Provocative Proposition for Working Relationships. "Mountain View College cultivates goodwill through positive and professional relationships with students, staff and the community. We value collaboration, integrity, service, mutual support and respect." This group then developed micro Provocative Propositions and Bold Ideas for realizing them.

Oakland Community College, Auburn Hills Campus, MI

> "Our intent was to move toward self-organization and continuity of change as organically as possible, allowing the participants themselves to discern, determine and direct our activities."

Lane Glenn, former dean of academic and student services at the Auburn Hills Campus of Oakland Community in Michigan, later became vice president of academic affairs at Northern Essex Community College in Massachusetts. At Auburn Hills, he facilitated a two-year Inquiry on the topic of Serving Students, Serving Ourselves for the multiple Student Services departments on the campus. The year before, the multiple departments had been relocated to the same building for the first time in the campus' history. More than 40 faculty and staff worked in these areas and were involved in the ongoing Inquiry.

Glenn first pulled together a Core Group or leadership team of four people to determine the focus of the Inquiry. The first meeting of the team involved an overview of AI and a paired interview using the generic AI Interview Guide (Watkins & Mohr, 2003, p. 99) to prime the pump and get everyone talking about what was working and what excited them in their respective areas of responsibility.

Glenn said, "We all recognized that we had a distinct advantage working in our favor as we approached our particular Appreciative Inquiry process: our work was not precipitated by budget cutbacks, a personnel crisis, reorganization, or any one of a number of other crises that might take an inordinate amount of attention and draw energy away from a positive focus." The team decided on the topic of Serving

Students, Serving Ourselves, with three intended outcomes: (1) exceptional service to students; (2) a happy work environment; and (3) encouraging teamwork.

Together, the leadership team created the timeline, modified the Interview Guide to make it specific to their topics and designed the workshop format that was used for the Appreciative Inquiry. To meet their own intended outcomes described above, they began with the assumption that the Inquiry process would initially be defined within a two-year timeline, with participants themselves determining if and where they should go after two years.

They decided to sponsor a series of workshops that fell into two categories: 1) half-day sessions that all faculty and staff would be encouraged to attend (supervisors would arrange for coverage and meals would be provided); and 2) Two-hour Brown Bags that all available and interested faculty and staff would be encouraged to attend (beverages and dessert provided). The timeline was:

Year One

September: "Serving Students, Serving Ourselves" Kick-off; all participants; 4 hours.
November: Student Services meeting; available participants; 2 hours.
January: "Serving Students, Serving Ourselves" Workshop; all participants; 4 hours.
March: Student Services meeting; available participants; 2 hours.
May: Student Services meeting; available participants; 2 hours.
July: Student Services meeting; available participants; 2 hours.

Year Two

September: "Serving Students, Serving Ourselves" Kick-off; all participants; 4 hours.
November: Student Services meeting; available participants; 2 hours.
January: "Serving Students, Serving Ourselves" Workshop; all participants; 4 hours.
March: Student Services meeting; available participants; 2 hours.
May: Student Services meeting; available participants; 2 hours.
July: Student Services meeting; available participants; 2 hours.

They assembled an agenda and Interview Guide for the kick-off session that would take participants through Discovery, Dream and Design in an initial half-day workshop. In the workshop, the large group divided into five small groups, each with representatives of multiple Student Services departments. Following the workshop, the Core Group collected and compiled the work of the five groups (their stories, themes, images of the future, Provocative Proposition statements, and individual and group Commitments, Gifts and Requests) and redistributed them to everyone in advance of a follow-up Brown Bag session.

Glenn said, "Our intent was to move toward self-organization and continuity of change as organically as possible, allowing the participants themselves to discern, determine and direct our activities."

As part of the pre-planning process, they agreed that they would allow the large group to determine the methods and process used for Destiny or Delivery. While they were open to "old paradigm" methods such as action planning, they hoped the group would move toward less traditional and less restrictive means of evolving the envisioned changes. As it turned out, the half-day workshop produced a wealth of paths they might choose to follow. They did some minor condensing (not reduction) of the work of the five groups, eliminating duplication and compiling everything into a single document, and used it as the basis for the follow-up Brown Bag session.

In this follow-up session (which drew nearly two-thirds of the original group of 40 - without the promise of a free meal!), the participants examined the full range of their: Provocative Proposition statements; Commitments, Gifts and Requests; and Initiatives. They decided to pull together some of their favored ideas into a few broad project categories. These included: (1) environment (aesthetics and user-friendliness of student services building and offices); communication (meetings, newsletters, web sites, events, leveraging technology and other issues related to optimizing communication with students, faculty and staff); and orientation (creating/revising orientation experiences tailored to specific student populations-for example, ESL students or Special Populations students). Specific Initiatives included aesthetics for the Student Services building, increased recruitment literature, more information-sharing opportunities, picture ID cards for students, collaborative teamwork, child care during student service opportunities and student access to services

Participants signed up for one or more of these project categories and were also invited to express interest in leadership roles for each. They agreed that the project teams would commence their work with the beginning of the next semester and they would use the planned half-day workshops and two-hour brown bags throughout the year to report progress, seek assistance as needed, redefine project work as appropriate and celebrate success whenever possible.

The members of the leadership team agreed to function as ongoing resources to the project teams, assisting with project clarification and, particularly, resource procurement as needed.

At the time of reporting, Glenn said that "two out of three of the leadership team's initial intended outcomes were well underway. Positive inter-departmental relationships are forming around project-based activity that provides us all with a comfortable, productive mechanism for coming together as a complete Student Services unit."

He also said, "The Appreciative Inquiry process is a natural and comfortable one for me - I'm a born optimist and a card-carrying Optimist (member of Optimists International). I'm constantly seeking the 'silver lining' in bad situations and encouraging positive communication and working methods in those around me. At the same time, I'm also a results-oriented planner, familiar and comfortable with 'traditional' planning methods (SWOT analyses, functional leadership roles, action plans, etc.) While I wholeheartedly embrace the underlying principles of Appreciative Inquiry, I have been a healthy skeptic about how it may produce results without specific, actionable and accountable planning methods."

Ohlone College, CA

Lesley Anne Buehler, Kay Harrison, Deb Parziale and Joanne Schultz, Ohlone College in California, co-facilitated an Appreciative Inquiry on the topic of New Ways of Working

> "Budget cuts had forced the department to do more with less. However, just trimming bodies didn't provide the information on how to redirect processes for the staff left behind."

Together: Enhancing Efficiency and Productivity for the Business Services department consisting of finance, purchasing, mailroom and duplicating services.

The group wanted to develop a department that was more team oriented and more connected to the vision of Ohlone College; they also wanted to develop a department that was more efficient, self

> "On-going success will be achieved simply because there will always be a new 'area' to investigate and keep the 'AI oil light' burning."

directing and that was recognized by other staff and faculty.

A pilot program involving the Business Services department was conducted. All department employees agreed to take part in this pilot and were aware of the needs for change and its possible outcomes. Schultz said, "Budget cuts had forced the department to do more with less. However just trimming bodies didn't provide the information on how to redirect processes for the staff left behind." The group created a Provocative Proposition that they all fully supported: "Focused on service, powered by people!"

The group committed to focusing on the following four elements when they thought of change in their department: teamwork, job enjoyment/satisfaction, professional development and continuous learning, and employee empowerment.

Schultz said, "The team planned to continue this process ad infinitum to ensure positive and continual change. Collect and convey all the valuable stories that arise out of the process changes. Change is continuous and necessary for growth.

"Celebration will be a matter of seeing GREAT results reflected on a graph, and/or posters on the campus walls; or of seeing the happy and proud attitudes of the groups involved. Having a PARTY! Ongoing success will be achieved simply because there will always be a new 'area' to investigate and keep the 'AI oil light' burning."

Initiatives included the creation of a department web page by a team of three and the development of an online requisition system available to all departments.

Buehler said, "I really liked the fact that no one lost focus of the goal to improve and work on the Business Services department for both AI sessions. It was also refreshing to hear the members who participated sharing their positive experience with others on campus after the events."

Harrison found "the group's energy both enjoyable and inspiring. I was impressed with their willingness to share ideas and their obvious excitement about returning to work to implement those ideas. In addition, I liked getting to know all of the people in this group and I came to appreciate their unique perspectives."

Parziale recalled, "My best experience was seeing the excitement and commitment of each of the participants and motivation to be involved to work toward a positive end. Now two months later, I continue to see the same enthusiasm and pride in work being accomplished to meet their goals."

Schultz concluded: "The VP of our department participated and it was great to have upper level support as well as witness the respect that she had for the staff and vice versa. Also the SEIU (Service Employees International Union) president participated, reluctantly, but it went so well he wants to bring this AI process to the rest of his unit."

*Planning*

## Amarillo College, TX

Patsy Lemaster, director of professional and organizational development at Amarillo College in Texas shared a story about an all-employee Conversation Day the College held. When Steve Jones became the new president there, he used the Day to kick off a strategic planning process. Formerly at a community college in Arkansas, Jones borrowed the concept of Conversation Day from The Higher Learning Commission's AQIP process. For details on AQIP, see Chapter Seven.

A series of conversations was facilitated, each focused on one of four questions: (1) What do we agree matters most? (2) What do we agree are our strengths - the aspects about Amarillo College that shine vibrantly? (3) What holds the greatest opportunity for making a significant difference at Amarillo College? and (4) What "Nikes" or must-do, easily done items would make a difference? More than 550 employees participated in small groups of six to eight people each.

As a result of the four conversations, Amarillo College employees identified: four common aspects that enabled employees to do their peak, most effective work; eight processes that mattered most for focus in the immediate future; eleven attributes that, if developed more fully, would make Amarillo College an even higher performance organization; evident strengths of the College in general; recent changes that have benefited students; evident strengths in collaboration; evident strengths of faculty, classified staff and administrators; 37 recommendations for making a significant difference in the near future; and 88 potential Nikes or quick-fix issues to address to improve college operations.

In the following months, Amarillo College prioritized the actions inspired by the conversation, using data about the organization and from other constituents, to build an environment that reflected those aspects of the culture that mattered most to employees' best work, to recognize and build on strengths, and to prioritize and address the Nike ideas for operational excellence.

## Colorado Community College System

A. Allen Butcher, unit administrator for Online Learning at the Community College of Denver's Southwest Campus at Teikyo Loretto Heights, was invited to facilitate an Inquiry for the Online Course Migration Team of the Colorado Community College System (CCCS). This was a group of 16 representatives of the online learning programs of the 13 regional community colleges comprising the CCCS.

CCCS's mission was to plan and, once the final decision was made, facilitate the consolidation of the online learning programs of all 13 colleges. Allen facilitated a session to help the group create a shared vision for the future based on its past and current successes and strengths. One of the inspired actions coming out of the Inquiry was an agreement to share best practices. That agreement, in turn, inspired the Quality Committee to commit to creating a template for the design and structure of all CCCS courses, based on what worked best for the various regional community colleges.

## Community College of Baltimore County, MD

Gayona Beckford-Barclay, assistant director of international education and multicultural learning, Office of Multicultural Affairs, and Kelly Lemons, coordinator of equity programming, both at the Community College of Baltimore County (CCBC), co-facilitated an Appreciative Inquiry on the topic of Global Education.

> "By the end of the day, some powerful ideas were created that would help increase global awareness."

The Inquiry involved a cross-section of participants from within CCBC as well as stakeholders from the local community. Participants said that they enjoyed the opportunity of getting to know people from different arenas, e.g., local government, community, etc. They also enjoyed going through the AI cycle, making significant connections, and coming up with Provocative Propositions and inspired action steps.

One of the Provocative Propositions they created was, "We dream of a world where the following is true: our institution is globally oriented; we are committed to developing true global citizens; language and culture are infused in all aspects of education; everyone has the opportunity of international exchange and experiential learning; and international understanding is fostered through profound international and intercultural experiences. Our goal is to achieve this dream."

A second Provocative Proposition was, "CCBC's commitment to Global Education fosters curricular and co-curricular experiences that build the relationships necessary to prepare students to be global citizens who can effectively participate in a complex and diverse society." CCBC used the Provocative Propositions as mission and vision statements in a Global Education Advisory Board Proposal document.

Beckford-Barclay and Lemons said that they were moved by the sharing of information among the groups. Additionally, there was a collective passion within the total group regarding intercultural competency as well as global awareness. "By the end of the day," they said, "some powerful ideas were created that would help increase global awareness."

## Community College of Baltimore County, MD

> " . . . I was able to witness the initial hesitancy slowly give way to enthusiasm and belief in the *possibility* of making a positive change within the majority of participants during the retreat."

Natalie Kimbrough, assistant professor in the history department at the Community College of Baltimore County (CCBC) in Maryland, co-facilitated a one-day retreat using Appreciative Inquiry for the Essex Campus' Career Services Department (CACS). Her co-facilitator was Judy Snyder, also at CCBC.

The director of CACS wanted to hold a retreat because, in his perception, members of the department had low morale, and there was a lack of teamwork and communication. Kimbrough and Snyder started the retreat with a video on virtual awareness followed by The Power of Words, a short video used in the AIFT. After a brief overview of AI, Kimbrough and Snyder co-facilitated the five generic processes of AI.

The department generated a number of life-giving forces for when the department was at its best: congeniality, opportunity for growth, autonomy and passion. The groups then created Provocative Propositions around these four themes, followed by Bold Ideas for the department as a whole and Commitments for individual members of the department.

Kimbrough said, "The sharing of images, Provocative Propositions, and the ideas really hit home with the group. The commitment and final part of the retreat was very stimulating as clear commitments were made and requests to be reminded of them by the person committing to a specific action."

According to Kimbrough, "The retreat seems to have impacted the majority of those who were present immediately. Some were understandably hesitant but all participated. It was interesting to see that some participants had hoped to use this retreat more as an 'airing out' of issues (some of the participants mentioned this directly to me. They mentioned initial hopes of getting to the real issues by attacking them directly, which included things such as 'this person always does . . . '). However, with some further explanation and guidance during the shared image (i.e., Provocative Propositions) phase, these participants realized the power of addressing the issues without focusing on the negative. That was very rewarding to see as it developed right in front of me with me only providing a little more guidance on the image phase.

" . . . I was able to witness the initial hesitancy slowly give way to enthusiasm and belief in the possibility of making a positive change within the majority of participants during the retreat. I have also been assured that the Internal Suggestion Box has become a part of the department's daily life.

"Personally facilitating this retreat was really groundbreaking. Since our training, I had tried to use AI in my direct environment, my department, but with mixed success. This mixed success was partially based on the crazy schedules that everyone has and partially on the fact that I did not make it an 'obvious' AI piece. Instead I was trying to implement AI by using what colleagues had told me they wanted more of. However, the commitment was lacking due to the scheduling issues. Therefore, seeing how this retreat did immediately impact the group of participants and the immediate effect it seemed to have been (was) very enlightening and rewarding to me. It also reminded me of the various aspects and ways in which AI can touch us on a daily basis. I mentioned before how impressed I was with seeing participants turn away from the 'blame game' and using their energy to illustrate the positives that they wish to have more of.

"The inquiry (topics are) a recurring theme it seems to me in many places: low morale due to lack of communication, feelings of not enough trust, and so forth. It is truly amazing to see that at the core most of us are looking for the same things and are driven by passion for what we do, while these characteristics seem to get lost along the way so often. Helping someone, a group, reclaim that and broaden that is truly rewarding.

"My best experience was . . . being able to refocus the negative energy into creating a positive image and helping the mindset of some of the participants to switch from the 'blame game' approach towards the AI approach, which happened right in front of me after I had been asked why we are not addressing the 'real' issues head-on. The other experience was to see the commitment in the majority of participants at the end. Some of the participants made commitments and asked for help from the rest of the group to enable them to keep that commitment. That was team-spirit and trust in action!"

## Community College of Baltimore County, MD

Karen Pell, president of VIA Consulting, Donna Reihl, director of extension at the Community College of Baltimore County (CCBC), and Kent Smedley, director of business and management at CCBC, co-facilitated an Inquiry for staff and students in CCBC's Commercial Vehicle Training (CVT) program. This non-credit College program operates on a self-sustaining basis to prepare students to be examined for a CDL-A (tractor trailer) or CDL-B (straight truck/bus) license.

> "We had people who did not want to leave. Our participants were truck drivers who, as one student stated: We thought it would be '...difficult to teach an old dog new tricks.' Not only did we teach new tricks, they were actively engaged, honest in their assessments and statements, positive in their outlooks, and had fun."

Smedley and a program assistant, who had not attended an AIFT, made up the Core Group, defining the topic and modifying the Interview Guide. The positive topic was Sustainable Growth for the CVT Program.

In the first phase, Pell and Reihl used a modified Interview Guide to interview student truck drivers by telephone. They summarized the themes that students reported to them in the interviews in a session with program staff and additional students, during which they participated in face-to-face interviews, using the same modified Interview Guide. That group then identified the life-giving forces in the system from all the interviews and, using that data, created a Provocative Proposition:

"We achieve our goals and growth and are the preferred provider of CDL training by effective teamwork and the support of our students through a commitment to student success, ethical behavior and job placement assistance, and the upgrading and integration of our facilities. We look for new and varied ways to successfully market our program and build relationships with transportation employers and our agency partners."

The group also developed a 'bumper sticker' - CCBC Rolling Towards the Future - two major Strategic Intentions and a variety of Individual Commitments to realize the Provocative Proposition. They also agreed on a number of ways to sustain the momentum generated by the Inquiry.

The trio of facilitators said that co-facilitating "turned out to be a great way to facilitate, and the outcomes were much better than we expected. Another wish was for a design for a three-year program plan to evolve from the process, and utilizing AI yielded an incredible amount of information and the planned growth of the program was a major outcome of the day. We each had a 'personal best': Kent's wish was to assist with planning, and Karen wanted to work through AI, as was Donna's to facilitate the learning. Donna also wanted to work with the 'goose egg' framework (Watkins & Mohr, 2003, p. 137-138) to cement this in her brain. The exercise worked very well and was an effective tool."

They said, "We had people who did not want to leave. Our participants were truck drivers who, as one student stated: We thought it would be '...difficult to teach an old dog new tricks.' Not only did we teach new tricks, they were actively engaged, honest in their assessments and statements, positive in their outlooks, and had fun.

We thought the visual metaphor activity in which we used toys, props, and craft supplies would be a hard sell, but they threw themselves into the project and did a terrific job. They got it, and they participated fully. It was a great day for all."

The Power of Words [DVD]. CRM Learning.

Stavros, J., D. Cooperrider & L. Kelley (2003). *Strategic inquiry > appreciative intent: inspiration to SOAR, a new framework for strategic planning.* London: AI Practitioner, November.

Watkins & Mohr (2003). *Appreciative inquiry for organization change: theory, practice and application.* Unpublished workshop resource book.

Whitney, D., D. Cooperrider, A. Trosten-Bloom, & B. Kaplin (2002). *Encyclopedia of Positive Questions* Euclid, OH: Lakeshore Communications.

# Chapter Five

## TEACHING AND LEARNING

Community colleges and other institutions of higher education are using Appreciative Inquiry (AI) to help teachers teach and learners learn. Two community colleges – Delta College in Michigan and SanJacinto College in Texas - and two four-year colleges – Le Moyne College and Nazareth College in New York - share their stories of success regarding the use of AI in teaching and learning.

### Delta College, MI

#### Background of the College

Delta College, in University Center, Michigan, serves Saginaw, Midland and Bay counties in east central Michigan. The College opened in 1961 and currently serves approximately 11,000 academic and skilled trades students. It is a charter member of the National League for Innovation in the Community College; Jean Goodnow is the president.

#### Introduction to AI

Leslie Prast and Connie Watson became trained as AI Facilitators in June 2004. Prast was a professor of English and director of the Center for Organizational Success at Delta College before her retirement in 2007. Watson was an instructor of psychology at Delta. After learning how to facilitate AI, they decided to team up and find ways of using it in the classroom to enhance teaching and learning. Here are several stories about their successes.

*Leslie Prast's Story*

> **"I know that the retention rate for students was higher in all the courses I used AI in, compared with previous classes."**

In Fall 2004 and beyond, Leslie Prast used AI on the first day of class to begin each of her developmental and advanced college composition courses. To make the process more inclusive, she did not distribute a course syllabus at the beginning of the course as she normally would; instead, she asked the students to partner with her in creating a great class together. That was the positive topic of Inquiry. The students seemed skeptical at first, but all were willing to go along and try out a new approach.

According to Prast, the paired interviews and small group dialogue in the AI cycle were fun for students, especially focusing on positive experiences of past great classes. To her surprise, only one student - out of about 150 total - said that he had never had a great class. When Prast asked if he had ever played sports in high school, he said yes, he had enjoyed success as a football player. She then asked him to remember a positive time in his football career when he had enjoyed a team learning or coaching experience and he found that he was easily able to relate a story from his experience as an athlete.

Prast said she was always excited to see the small-group Dream Statements and Strategies the students created to make the class great for all of them. They frequently described Strategies that Prast usually would have included in her syllabus anyway: attend regularly and on time; come with the assignment prepared; ask questions; be open to new ideas, etc. However, creating the Strategies themselves from their own best experiences of past great classes gave students the confidence to know that they could create a great class together and also inspired them to take the actions they developed because they owned them. In all classes, the most successful Strategy students recalled was collaborating on group projects and assignments, an easy one for Prast to facilitate.

All the students took AI seriously; none developed Strategies for having "no homework" or "canceling class." However, Prast found that good communication was necessary to maintain a partnership relationship between the students and the teacher. For example, the students would sometimes try to put the responsibility on Prast for making sure their Dream Statements were realized. In those cases, she would throw the ball back into their court and ask them how "we" were going to work together to implement the Strategies and realize the Dream Statements.

In one instance, one class identified the Strategy of "reasonable work load" for Prast to implement. Her response was to ask them what "reasonable" meant and how she would know whether the work she was assigning was "reasonable" for them or not. As a result, they had a good discussion about the importance of good communication between students and instructor. They all promised to collaborate in setting and keeping assignment deadlines while still achieving the content and skills of the student learning outcomes. In the end, they all agreed to add the phrase "communicate needs" to the "reasonable work load" Strategy.

Another example of partnering was the Strategy, "Learn everyone's name," which was suggested in several classes. Again, Prast asked the students to devise a way for students to learn each other's names. One student suggested a method that someone had used in a previous course Prast said, "It was fun and worked very well." They then were able to call everyone by their first names, contributing to the sense of community and cooperation in the class.

*Check In at Midterm.* Around midterm each semester in each course, Prast asked students how they were doing in terms of implementing the Strategies for achieving their Dream Statements. While almost all of the feedback was positive, she also received information that allowed her to address a certain classroom "problem" from a positive frame. She had been wondering how to deal with a well-meaning student who was dominating class discussions by calling out answers and generally acting as the class spokesperson. At the midterm check in, when she asked students, "What should be changed?", they said: "Be respectful," "Pay attention during presentations," and "Wait your turn to speak." Interestingly, the talkative student countered by suggesting that his classmates do more to "Contribute to the MAX," as he felt that he was doing all the work. The discussion created an opportunity to focus on how each student could take responsibility for contributing to class discussions, since some readily admitted that they were only too happy to sit back and let their talkative classmate make all the effort.

In another class, when Prast asked the students at midterm, "Is this a great class yet?", two of the three student groups responded, "Yes!" while the third group said, "It is an OK, no big deal class (we are not all tight yet)." This intriguing answer led Prast to ask more questions about what this group meant. It turned out that the classroom-seating configuration was a problem for this particular group seated at long tables in rows facing the teacher at the front of the classroom, they were unable to see their classmates during class. This was news to Prast, since the seating worked well from her perspective; she was able to see all the students while having them see both her and the whiteboard behind her. As a result of the discussion, they decided to rearrange the tables into a "U" shape around the outside of the room, so that the students could see each other, as well as Prast and the board. This group decision changed the whole dynamic of the class, making for a friendlier environment, helping the students feel more comfortable with each other and demonstrating the teacher's willingness to collaborate with them and to respect their ideas and opinions about their preferred learning environment.

*Improved Retention and Final Grades.* Prast said, "I know that the retention rate for students was higher in all the courses I used AI in, compared with previous classes" (Prast, 2007). From Fall 2003 to Winter 2004, prior to using AI, the average retention rate for all of Prast's classes and sections was 87.8 percent; after using AI, the average retention rate was 89.8 percent - an improvement of 2 percentage points overall. Prast believes that retention was improved because students looked out for each other, formed friendships and contributed to each other's successful learning. For instance, when a student was absent, at least one classmate would call or email to give a review of what was covered in class and what was assigned for the next class meeting. This was possible because they had decided to exchange telephone numbers and email addresses for this purpose.

Final grades improved as well. For Fall 2003 and Winter 2004, before Prast began using AI, the average of the final grades for English 90, Developmental English–Introduction to College Reading and Writing - was 75.8 percent. For Fall 2004 and Winter 2005, after beginning to use AI, the average of the final grades was 79.8 percent - an improvement of 4 percentage points. For Fall 2003 and Winter 2004, the average final grades for English 112, College Composition II, was 79.9 percent and, after using AI, 83.1 percent - an improvement of 3.2 percentage points (Prast, 2007).

By their own admission, students in AI classes looked forward to coming to class and working together instead of competing with each other and Prast was happy to adopt a less authoritarian role. By allowing the students to create their own "great class" based on the best of their past experiences, she was able to produce a course syllabus that reflected student ideas from their individual and group past successes.

Another example of student empowerment engendered by AI was the initiative that students took in reminding each other of a particular Strategy, e.g., "Be respectful" or "Be open-minded with a positive attitude toward others' ideas" if or when someone made a put-down comment about another classmate's contribution, question, or answer.

*More Rewarding for the Teacher.* Prast said that using AI in her classes made teaching more rewarding and enjoyable for her by enlisting the collaboration and positive energy of her students to envision, design and implement great classes together.

## Connie Watson's and Leslie Prast's Story

Beginning in Fall 2004, Connie Watson and Leslie Prast implemented AI at the beginning of their own classes each semester to help students create great classes. In addition, they also introduced ways of using AI in the classroom to full and part-time faculty at Delta College at the start of each semester so that they might also use AI to collaboratively create great classes.

To help faculty easily get on board with AI, Watson and Prast developed several handouts. They also developed questions for use at midterm to get feedback from students on how the course was working out. See Appendices at the end of this story for easily reproduced handouts.

According to Watson and Prast, more and more Delta College faculty are using AI at the start of their classes and expressing interest in AI. They learned that faculty and students, in developmental to advanced courses across disciplines, share the desire for a rewarding class and they eagerly commit to AI as a means of creating and achieving their shared Dreams.

*Prast's Composition II English Class.* Following are some examples of Dream Statements created by students in Prast's Composition II English class in Fall 2004:

We are interacting with others on interesting topics in a relaxed atmosphere while applying it to life!

In this class we work hard towards achieving a successful life.

In this class, we work together to make it a relaxed atmosphere so that the class is interesting and it applies to our lives.

In ENG 112 we are relaxed and interested while applying what we learn to life as well as applying ourselves.

We work and learn interactively in a relaxed atmosphere from a great teacher with interesting topics that apply to life!

Here are some examples of Strategies that students developed in order to actualize their Dream Statements:

Attitude: dedication/devotion to achieving goals
Open to others' ideas
Communicate likes and hobbies
Creative teaching: variety of activities, students teach each other
Work together on group projects
Strong work ethic/organization
Controversial topics to promote different views
Take responsibility for learning/getting the most out of the class
Conference with the teacher
Regular attendance
Reasonable work load (communicate needs)
Make connections to our own lives
Learn everyone's name

*Midterm Check In.* At midterm, Prast asked students two questions: What is working well for us? And "What should be changed, i.e., what do we want more of?" Some results from College Comp II appear below:

What is working well for us?

Interaction between classmates
Have incorporated many of our strategies while working on our group research projects
Assignments on board at end of every class
Everyone involved
Pace of class
Good work load and positive atmosphere

What should be changed? (What do we want more of?)

Group work?
Breakfast buffet with omelet chef!
Less dream statement work

More group projects with different people to get to know others better
Nothing

Is this a great class yet? Why or why not?

We are on our way.
Yes, everyone seems to know each other and we are meeting our strategies.
Yes, we are reaching our goals.
Yes, it is very interactive.
Yes. We are on track with our goals and we're having a great time here!

Here's what Tanya, a student in Prast's English class, had to say:

I believe the (Dream) statement had an impact on us to succeed by coming together as a group, by stating what type of class we all liked to have, and it gave us an incentive to work and do well in the class . . . I believe this activity was a useful resource to any class and I would recommend that more teachers use this concept.

*Connie Watson's Psychology Class*

Some examples of Dream Statements from Watson's psychology class, Fall 2006 include the following:

Having hands on experience is a life full of commitment.

We strive everyday to stay committed to our goals and classmates by creating a fun, hands on environment that is applied to our everyday lives.

We are committed to using hands-on class experience with psychology and applying it to our daily lives.

We are committed to a hands-on learning experience that we can apply to real life.

Here are some examples of Strategies developed by the students:

Be on time to achieve our commitment
Keep up with current issues
Do the things that are asked of you
Good classroom discussions on what we have learned
Be open with hands on ideas
Relate assignments to your life
We will all have positive attitudes to promote a healthy learning environment for everyone
Not skipping class (i.e., attending class)
Paying attention
Staying involved in group activities/questions
Bringing life experiences inside the classroom

## Appendix A

### Process for Using Appreciative Inquiry (AI) in the Classroom

In the first class meeting, invite students to partner with you in collaboratively creating a "great class" this term. The time for each activity can be designed to fit the length of the class; for one-hour classes, you might need to take two full sessions or assign some of the activities as an out-of-class activity. For instance, once students have chosen partners for the paired interviews, the interviews themselves could take place outside of class.

Explain briefly the Five Generic Processes of AI as a preview of the activity; you can project these on an overhead:

| Five Generic Processes of Appreciative Inquiry |
| :--- |
| 1. Choose the positive as the focus of inquiry |
| 2. Inquire into exceptionally positive moments |
| 3. Share the stories and identify life-giving forces |
| 4. Create shared images of a preferred future |
| 5. Innovate and improvise ways to create that future |

Ask the students to pair up with someone they don't know or don't know well. (If there is an uneven number, you can pair up with one of the students; this is more effective than having a trio). Tell them that they will be interviewing each other, using an Interview Guide that will help them share their stories about their best great-class experiences.

Allow time (20-30 miutes) for the interviews. Then ask them to turn over the Interview Guide, reflect on what they have heard from their partner and fill out the Summary Sheet.

Ask pairs to combine with one or two other pairs - students they don't know or don't know well - either four or six students per group, depending on the number of students in the class. Have each student share their partner's best stories, then brainstorm the themes they heard in the stories that created a "great class" in the past or present. Have each group discuss and choose the three to five themes they heard and record them on a piece of poster paper and hang or post it on the wall. Then someone from each group can present their themes to the class and ask if there are any questions about the meaning of the themes.

Hand out three colored sticky dots to all students and ask them to place sticky dots on the three themes that they personally think are essential to creating a "great class." Assure them that they are not voting; they are only graphically displaying the energy of the entire class.

Ask each small group to select one essential theme (with sub-themes if desired) that they all agree on (again, not voting but agreeing through dialogue) and create a Dream statement that synthesizes the themes or, through dialogue, generates new ones. This Dream Statement is positive and expressed in present tense and can be more than one sentence. Have each group write their Dream Statement on poster paper and hang it up or post it to present to the class.

If there's time, ask for one person from each of the small groups to come together and synthesize the various Dream Statements into one statement for the whole class; other students might take a short break. Or, keep the individual groups' Dream Statements, without synthesizing them. In either case, ask the students (still in small groups) to propose Strategies for making their Dream Statements become a reality. Have them record the Strategies under the Dream Statements and report them out to the whole class.

*Who is Responsible?*

Ask the students, who is responsible for making all this happen? They usually will answer, "We are." For example: "Learn everyone's name" was one Strategy. Ask the students for ideas on how to accomplish that. Show the students that they are partners with you in making this a "great class."

Input the Dream Statement(s) and Strategies into a word document, print a copy for each student, then hand them back to the students with the class syllabus at the next class meeting.

*Midterm Check In*

Around midterm, revisit the Dream Statements and Strategies. Put the students back into their original groups and ask them the following questions:

What is working well for us?

What do we need to change? What do we want MORE of?

Is this a "great class" yet? Why or why not?

Share and discuss the answers as a whole group. Discuss and agree on any desired changes.

## Appendix B

### Example of an Interview Guide for Creating a Great Class

**1. BEST EXPERIENCE**

A. Tell me about the most challenging and exciting class you ever had. What was it? What made it challenging and exciting? What did the teacher do? What did you do? What did other students do?

B. How do you learn best? Tell me about a time when you learned something very challenging. What contributed to your learning?

C. Tell me about a class in which you learned a lot. What was the situation? Who else was involved and what did they do? What did you do to foster your own learning? What made this a highpoint learning experience for you?

**2. VALUES:**

A. Without being humble, what do you value most about yourself – as a person and as a learner?

B. When you are feeling best about learning, what about the act of learning do you value?

C. What do you value most about being a successful learner?

D. What is the single most important thing that contributes to your successful learning?

**3. THREE WISHES:** What three wishes do you have for this course?

## Appendix C

### Example of a Summary Sheet

1. BEST EXPERIENCES

What were the high-point stories that your partner shared with you about great classes and/or teaching and learning?

2. VALUES

What were the high-point values that your partner shared with you about great classes and/or teaching and learning?

3. THREE WISHES:

What were your partner's three wishes for this course?

San Jacinto College, TX

Background of the College

San Jacinto College is a community college with 22,000 credit students in southeast Houston, Texas. The College has three campuses. It is an Hispanic-serving, open-door institution with approximately five percent growth each semester. William Lindemann is the Chancellor of the College; the campus presidents are: Linda Watkins, South Campus, recently retired; Charles Grant, North Campus; and Monte Blue, Central Campus.

Introduction to AI

Dr. Linda Watkins participated in an Appreciative Inquiry Facilitator Training (AIFT©) in Eugene, Oregon in June 2005. When she returned to her campus, she identified six visionary faculty members from across the district who became the Core Group that helped Watkins plan her first Appreciative Inquiry; she facilitated the process, then went on to document it and become certified as an AI Facilitator. Later, she took a team of more than a dozen people from South Campus to participate in another AIFT in Houston in November 2005, including Ann Tate, a well-respected faculty member whom Watkins recruited to play a major role in bringing an appreciative approach to change to South Campus. Tate later assumed a College-wide role.

> "The process of Appreciative Inquiry gave us recognition by focusing on what we do best. I appreciate this recognition and I feel renewed as the semester gets underway."

Watkins oriented the original team of seven to AI with overviews, videos and handouts for 16 hours. This Core Group of seven was responsible for identifying the positive topic or topics of the Inquiry; designing the Inquiry for use with a larger group; and modifying the generic Interview Guide to the specific topic or topics for the Inquiry.

The Core Group identified Reenergizing Teaching and Learning Across the District as the positive topic because that's what they wanted to create more of. The group then selected 30 visionary faculty members across the district to serve as the Inquiry group.

The orientation to the interviews started with the question: "Tell me a story about a deep learning experience you have had in your life." Then the Inquiry group used the modified Interview Guide in paired, face-to-face interviews; see Appendix D. After sharing each other's high-point stories, they brainstormed the life-giving forces from the stories for reenergizing teaching and learning at the College.

Here are the themes they discovered:

Mutual respect between faculty/students, faculty/administration, faculty/faculty
Enthusiasm among faculty
Fairness between all parties
Passion about subject matter
Engaged students
Empathetic listening to one another
Passion for student success
Passion for teaching and learning
Personal touch
Administrative respect of faculty
Positive attitudes
Support for one another
Empowering faculty to innovate and trusting faculty to exceed expectations
Working together toward common goal
Recognition

From those themes, the Inquiry group then created a Dream Statement or Provocative Proposition: "San Jacinto College faculty is re-energizing teaching and learning across the district. The College offers leading-edge and dynamic instructional programming in an environment that is built upon mutual respect, continued learning and passion for what we do."

The Inquiry group then created Strategic Initiatives for realizing the Dream:

1. Develop a Center for Excellence for Teaching and Learning, to include opportunities for professional development, new faculty orientation, leadership development, and mentoring. The district-wide Center for Excellence in Teaching and Learning will focus on opportunities for renewal and growth and strategies to re-energize teaching and learning.
2. Develop opportunities for recognition of excellent teaching and learning (i.e., a Faculty Fellows program).
3. Develop opportunities for faculty/administrators/staff to come together socially as well as professionally in order to build a sense of collegiality, mutual respect, and community.

## Outcomes of the Inquiry

The three Strategic Initiatives garnered the support of administration and were funded for $100,000 in 2005-06. The team requested additional funding of $270,000 for 2006-07 and the administration remained committed to the Initiatives.

> **"I recommend that administrators and faculty across the nation embrace the Appreciative Inquiry approach."**

Best-practice visits were conducted throughout the state and nation as they related to the Strategic Initiatives. Also, best-practice stories from across the San Jacinto College District were elicited. The College then created a best-practice video.

Spring 2006 Faculty In-service Day continued the Inquiry: Re-energizing Teaching and Learning across the San Jacinto College District. Six reassigned faculty designed and coordinated the continuing Inquiry. Faculty members were energized and provided input for implementing the Strategic Initiatives.

The initiatives became totally faculty-driven. Tate was reassigned as the campus director of the Center of Excellence for Teaching and Learning to direct the initiatives. She later became the College Director of the Professional Development Center. Growing out of the three Strategic Initiatives, she added a new semester-long faculty orientation program, a Leadership Development Program for faculty and staff, and a continued Faculty Fellows program that supports Centers for Excellence on each of the three campuses. The Director has a staff of three and three faculty fellows.

The Core Group celebrated its first milestone of success at an off-campus luncheon and planned to keep Appreciative Inquiry alive with continued focus groups, surveys, dialogue and expanded opportunities for growth and development.

According to one faculty member, "The process of Appreciative Inquiry gave us recognition by focusing on what we do best. I appreciate this recognition and I feel renewed as the semester gets underway."

## Impact: An Appreciative Approach to Teaching and Learning

Watkins said, "With the funding cuts and challenges facing community colleges today, it is my belief that faculty respond and are motivated by a positive focus and vision. Often we focus on the negatives rather than on the synergy that makes the community college the exciting place that it is. I recommend that administrators and faculty across the nation embrace an appreciative approach to teaching and learning. Also, it is my belief that projects related to teaching and learning be faculty driven."

Appendix D

Interview Guide

1. In each of our lives, there are special times when we just know that we have made the right career choice - moments when we feel really good about the work we are doing and what we are contributing to others. As you think back over your time at San Jacinto College, tell me a story about one of those special moments when you felt that your teaching was really alive and meaningful for your students.
What made it an exciting experience?
Who else was involved?
How were you interacting with your students?
What was it about the instructional environment that made it so special?
Give an example of an exceptionally great instructor.
Give an example of the best learning experience you have ever had.

2. Tell me a story about an experience you had at San Jacinto College in which you felt the college administration supported you in teaching and learning.
What made it an exciting experience?
How did you feel this support made you a better teacher?
How did this experience lead to further interaction/discussion with other faculty?
How did your students benefit from your experience?
Give an example of an exceptionally great administrator.

3. Without being humble, what do you value most about your contributions to teaching?
What makes you an outstanding instructor?
Why do you think you are an outstanding instructor?
When you are feeling best about your work, what do you value about it?

4. In working with fellow faculty, one thing that enables great teaching/learning is when people in the college feel connected or part of a family. Thinking back over the past years, tell me about a time when you felt the college was a family or community.
What role did you play?
What role did other faculty play?
What role did the administration play?
What other factors contributed to this environment of connectedness?
Give an example when all three SJC campuses worked well together.
Give an example of a department or a division at San Jacinto College that works well as a team. What factors do you think contribute to the teamwork of that department or division?

5. With the hectic pace of a semester and the other obligations that surround your life, feeling valued and supported by those that are around you make a big difference. Relate a story about a specific time, an experience when, as a professional, you felt genuinely supported and/or valued by students, by your peers, or by the administration.

6. What three wishes do you have for this College – things that would enable it to become even more vibrant and truly the sort of place in which great learning and teaching take place on a daily basis?

Le Moyne College and Nazareth College, NY

> **"A 'fuller' and (more) hopeful view of the future - images of what students can be - emerges as an alternative to an 'empty' view - what they should not be."**

In response to the question, how can excellence in the classroom be attained?, college management professors and authors Dennis O'Connor of Le Moyne College in Syracuse, NY, and the late Leodones Yballe of Nazareth College of Rochester, NY, answered: through a pedagogy of appreciation. O'Connor earned his Ph.D. in Organizational Behavior at Case Western Reserve University, the birthplace of Appreciative Inquiry; David Cooperrider, chief architect of AI, was a professor in the program.

Like Appreciative Inquiry, Appreciative Pedagogy involves a way of viewing the world that is at once realistic, positively transforming and hopeful. It is realistic because the focus of inquiry and source of vision is the abundant experience of the learners. It is positively transforming because it radically changes experience from irrelevance and boredom to one of high energy, connectedness and importance. It is hopeful because what is apprehended engenders positive images of the future that can guide action and transform current realities of the participants (2004, p. 175).

Relationship between Experiential Learning and Appreciative Pedagogy

The authors believed that Appreciative Pedagogy (AP) could "complement and extend" the power of David Kolb's cycle of experiential learning (1984). Also a professor of Organizational Behavior at Case Western, Kolb's cycle includes four phases of experiential learning: concrete experience; reflective observation; abstract conceptualization; and active experimentation.

The two-part Discovery phase of the AI cycle, (1) inquire into exceptionally positive moments and (2) share the stories and identify life-giving forces, is similar to Kolb's concrete experience and reflective observation phases. Inquirers are first asked to share stories about their best experiences in an interview related to the topic of inquiry and then, in groups, reflect on the themes that the stories have in common. By recalling their positive-moment stories, inquirers are re-generating their experiences "as if" they were happening in the moment as concrete experiences. By sharing their stories with others and generating the themes that are common or most exciting, they are reflecting on their own and others' concrete experiences.

The Dream phase of the AI cycle, create shared images of a preferred future, is similar to the abstract conceptualization phase of experiential learning. Inquirers are asked to generate a Provocative Proposition, or shared vision, of what it would look like if they were experiencing their high-point moments all or more of the time.

The Design and Destiny phases of the AI cycle innovate and improvise ways to create that future and are similar to the active experimentation phase in that they ask inquirers to generate inspired actions for realizing their shared visions and to continue to improvise actions that will make the visions real.

## Discovery

> "... energy tends to be heightened and more productively invested when directed towards discovery of what works rather than what does not work."

In the Discovery phase of AP, students discover - by recalling their own concrete best experiences of a particular topic, e.g., 'great teams' - the life-giving forces that support great teams. O'Connor and Yballe called this "inside-out learning," with the personal discoveries deepened by reading about team-building theories. Students share their stories, then discover the themes that are common among the stories, i.e., cohesion, shared leadership, consensus, integrity, etc.

The authors noted that the students often generated 90 percent or more of what expert readings on a certain topic would cover, although, they noted, it was unorganized. The professors then helped students sort out the themes, e.g., into those that were task-related and those that were relationship-related.

In addition to the topic of 'great teams,' other topics of inquiry in the classroom included peak performance, extraordinary motivation, exemplary leadership, core values and deep commitment. Yballe and O'Connor also used variations of AP to "explore and build competencies of various kinds," such as active listening. The idea was to discover and focus attention on peak experiences and life-giving forces. They argued that "energy tends to be heightened and more productively invested when directed towards discovery of what works rather than what does not work" (2004, p. 183).

## Dream

In the Dream phase of AP, students create Provocative Propositions or Dream Statements about the topic, drawing upon the themes they generated in the Discovery phase. Student groups then signed off on their statements in order "to establish a psychological contract." O'Connor and Yballe also had their students create a "motto" based on the Dream Statement. Here's what one student, Sarah, had to say about the Dream phase:

We used everything from our list of Best Team Characteristics. For example, we all agreed our team will be fun, productive where we all learn a lot about ourselves and relevant topics. We actually made it happen. I have never been part of a team where the members talked and went out together outside of class . . . I would describe my team as caring, fun, productive, focused, open-minded . . . I learned a lot about both myself and topics discussed in class . . . rewarding, and insightful. I could say a lot more but I don't have enough space in the form. (p. 185)

Yballe and O'Connor found other opportunities for an appreciative approach to pedagogy. For instance, in debriefing a corporate ethics role play, students were asked: "Where did examples of moral leadership occur? What made these possible? Have there been times in life when we exercised moral leadership at work or in other settings? What are the key factors necessary for personal and corporate moral leadership?" (p. 185).

Students were asked to identify personal leadership behaviors to help their team move towards the ideal, i.e., the Dream. Again, mirroring Kolb's learning cycle, students were asked to reflect and act:

> How are we doing so far in realizing our propositions and plans? What is going well? What have I done? What leadership or action is needed? What would be great to do? What is the first step to take from here, specifically? What will I do? (p. 186).

Students were also asked to generalize their answers to work and life situations beyond the class. O'Connor and Yballe also noted that

> While these steps have been presented as a sequential model, there are not always clear lines between discovering, dreaming, designing, and delivering (or achieving destiny) in practice. Inquiry and dialogue, particularly in groups, have a life of their own and are more of a dance, than a rigidly controlled prescription. (p. 187).

From their teaching and learning experiences, Yballe and O'Connor summed up the impact of Appreciative Pedagogy:

> We have observed more energized and sustained interactions . . . Students feel a sense of safety when publicly speaking up; they experience less fear and inhibitions . . . A positive attitude emerges towards other students as knowledgeable, trustworthy, and real . . . Students gain a greater trust in self and heightened confidence in their experience . . . Many students report a positive attitude toward the professor as resource, guide, and helper . . . Concepts and insights are personally meaningful and relevant because they are firmly rooted in personal experiences . . . A "fuller" and hopeful view of the future (images of what students can be) emerges as an alternative to an "empty" view (what they should not be) . . . Students begin to gain skill and confidence in Appreciative Inquiry as a creative alternative to objective analysis or problem solving . . . There have been positive consequences for us, the professors, when we have managed our classes with an appreciative stance (p. 187).

O'Connor and Yballe also expressed their own need to change, grow and learn from their experiences.

> The appreciative approach calls for a very different skill set than the traditional lecture style. Mistakes, uncertainty, resistance, and doubt are inevitable. Appreciative Pedagogy is a serious challenge. If you believe that it is possible, however, begin by looking for opportunities for small experiments. We believe that the positive results will kindle a long-term adventure for those willing to try (p. 191).

Yballe and O'Connor believed that "Students need not be just containers of knowledge, but can be partners in the re-creation and refinement of their society's knowledge and wisdom" (p. 191).

References for Chapter Five

Kolb, D. (1984). *Experiential learning*. Englewood Cliffs, NJ: Prentice Hall.

Prast, L. (2007). Personal email to author, September 7.

Yballe, L. & D. O'Connor (2004). Toward a Pedagogy of Appreciation. *Constructive Discourse and Human Organization*, edited by D. Cooperrider & M. Avital. Elsevier Science.

Yballe, L. & D. O'Connor (2000). Appreciative Pedagogy: Constructing Positive Models for Learning. *Journal of Management Education*, v. 24., n. 4. Thousand Oaks, CA: Sage Publications.

# Chapter Six

## HUMAN RESOURCE DEVELOPMENT

Six community colleges reported using Appreciative Inquiry for human resource development: conflict resolution, hiring and professional development. These colleges were: Lansing Community College in Michigan; Centralia College in Washington State; Asnuntuck Community College in Connecticut; Corning Community College in New York; Delta College in Michigan; and South Piedmont Community College in North Carolina.

*Conflict Resolution*

Lansing Community College, MI

| **"Trust this process!"** | Pam Bergeron, recently retired employee relations director for |

Pam Bergeron, recently retired employee relations director for Lansing Community College (LCC), Michigan, participated in an Appreciative Inquiry Facilitator Training (AIFT©), then facilitated an unusual and highly successful Appreciative Inquiry at LCC. Pam used a conflict resolution model for working with two people that was developed by Jennifer Mann, counselor at Santa Rosa Junior College in California. Bergeron successfully facilitated the resolution of a long-time conflict between two employees - a manager and someone the manager supervised.

Both employees agreed to try to resolve the conflict. Bergeron then gave them the Conflict Resolution Guide that contained four questions; both parties were asked to answer all questions fully before the first face-to-face meeting.

The trio met six times over a period of three months; in one of the sessions, Bergeron asked them to collaboratively develop a Provocative Proposition. According to Bergeron, when the pair first started to meet, "It was utterly painful." Bergeron's words again: "By the last meeting, they walked into the meeting room together and were laughing about something that had happened in the department that morning. When I asked them to appreciate this moment, and remember back three short months ago, they both looked at me like, what's the big deal? We always got along!"

Tangible outcomes of the Inquiry were: the 23-year veteran employee retained her job; the manager became interested in AI and borrowed source material; the manager began treating all employees in her area with a greater degree of respect; and the manager herself reports that she feels much healthier and calmer at work. Bergeron's best learning was, "Trust this process!"

Conflict Resolution Guide (courtesy of Jennifer Mann, Santa Rosa Junior College, CA)
(Give to the two individuals who are in conflict to complete, prior to a face-to-face consultation)

*Reflections in preparation for consultation*

Please consider these questions and make notes on a separate sheet prior to arriving at our meeting on _____ at _____. I understand that the goal of meeting is to act on your willingness to elicit agreements for a more harmonious working relationship. I salute you both!

1) Describe a time when you worked in a situation that was completely harmonious. What were the conditions and circumstances that created a feeling of harmony and collegiality? Make a lengthy list.

2) From the list above, select three qualities that are important to you in any working relationship and define them thoroughly.

3) Describe ANYTHING that is working about your current work relationship. Try to make a list here too.

4) Describe what you would like MORE OF as you continue to work with this person. Thank you for taking time to reflect on these questions. I look forward to meeting together.

*Hiring*

## Centralia College, WA

Rich Henry, Unified Field Associates, shared this story about appreciative hiring. In Spring 2004, Centralia launched a year-long effort to learn about and apply AI methods. The project was called Living Our Vision and focused on four large high-priority projects as the vehicles for learning: appreciative hiring, participatory governance, community connection and employee recognition.

> "These are the 13 best hires I've ever made. Every one of them is outstanding."

Living Our Vision was launched with a two-day training in April 2004 to both teach AI and to apply AI to get a significant start on each of the four projects. Appreciative hiring had the most urgent time horizon. Centralia was going to be hiring for 13 positions, beginning immediately.

Recognizing that getting clear about what they wanted more of was the first step, the appreciative hiring workgroup started by inquiring into the characteristics that people wanted in members of their college community. They interviewed each other and located the themes, resulting in a list of 37 desired characteristics, including such qualities as honest, articulate, innovative, life-long learner and compassionate.

Next they designed Appreciative Interview questions to elicit stories that would indicate a candidate's capacity for these qualities. Questions were mapped to the particular qualities that would most likely be revealed. For example, "Tell us about a time when you turned a difficult interaction into a positive experience" would likely reveal qualities of civility, creativity and embracing of diversity. "Describe a time when you experienced significant personal growth" would provide information for life-long learner, professionalism and being open to new ideas. Questions were combined to ensure that all or most of the 37 desired qualities would have the opportunity to emerge. Perhaps the most important difference between these appreciative questions and typical interview questions was that they invited deep, multi-faceted stories, rather than brief, perfunctory answers.

As part of the year-long AI process at Centralia, Henry and others conducted an evaluation (using Appreciative Inquiry methods) of results from the appreciative hiring changes. This included interviews of key college personnel and the newly hired people. The College president reported that this process was significantly different from any hiring process he'd been part of before and that he learned things about the candidates that he could not have learned in a typical interview. He said, "These are the 13 best hires I've ever made. Every one of them is outstanding."

The vice president of human resources identified three categories of assessment for every hire: knowledge, skills and abilities; "soft" skills like collaboration and communication; and how well the person would "fit" into the College's culture. The vice president said, "Structured interviews provide pretty good assessment of knowledge, skills and abilities, but don't generally do well for soft skills. Our appreciative process revealed a fuller range of the whole person."

The vice president of instruction noted, "This appreciative process let us see the real person beyond the resume. Being good at playing the interview game is very different than being good at the job. This process gave us a much better view into who would be best at the job. In almost every case, the committee, the president, and I came to the same conclusion independently. This process left no questions about who would be best for our college."

> **"When the interview was over, I knew I would absolutely take this position, if offered, despite the fact that I had two other applications out. It was a fundamental shift from anything I'd ever been through before."**

The new hires also found the experience atypical and very positive. One person said, "Of all the interviews I've been through, this one was the most comprehensive and personalized. And it got to the point where the details of my credentials were less relevant and they were more concerned about me as a person and a potential colleague. And this was utterly unique in any interview process I've been through. When the interview was over, I knew I would absolutely take this position, if offered, despite the fact that I had two other applications out. It was a fundamental shift from anything I'd ever been through before."

Another reported, "I had an opportunity to honestly let them know me, my character, my values, my beliefs, more than I've ever had the opportunity to share before. I felt absolutely certain that if they hired me, they were hiring *me*, and if they didn't hire me, it would be because it wasn't a good fit and that would be OK."

Someone else said, "In some application processes it feels like they're trying to ferret out my flaws. This was much more like a conversation with like-minded people who share values - how do I practice my teaching philosophy. It seemed they were trying to ferret out my strengths."

From the perspectives of both the College and the candidates, the key outcome seemed to be a much more accurate assessment of "fit." A second, less obvious benefit was that the candidates felt the interview process was actually the beginning of a deep relationship with the College. Their inclusion and integration with the college community began before their first day on the job, making that critical step all the more welcoming and transparent.

*Professional Development*

Asnuntuck Community College, CT

Susan Dantino, associate dean of institutional planning and effectiveness at neighboring Tunxis Community College in Connecticut, facilitated an Appreciative Inquiry retreat for Asnuntuck Community College's seven-member Executive Team at the request of Asnuntuck President

> **"My 'personal best' experience . . . was in seeing and having a part in facilitating the subtle transformation that occurred with individuals who moved from adversarial to thoughtfully reflective to recognition during the process."**

Martha McLeod. The positive topic for Inquiry was Exemplary College Leadership.

Dantino began the one-day retreat with questions that engaged participants in identifying things that made them laugh out loud within the past week, the best thing that happened within the week, what it felt like and an exercise to gain entrance into heaven by answering the question, "What gift do I bring with me into heaven?" followed by an exercise that demonstrated the power of the mind.

Dantino then provided a brief theoretical basis for AI: basic concepts, five core principles, five generic processes, terminology that would be used during the day and a Parking Lot, a piece of flip chart paper where topics that were not on the agenda could be parked for later discussion. The parking lot topics

80

were addressed after lunch, after Dantino re-framed the issues into what the group wanted more of, not less of.

Members of the team paired up and interviewed each other, using the following questions that had been prepared in advance.

1. Tell me a story about a time in your life when you were at your best as a college leader, where you led one or more people to make a positive difference. What did you do or say? What excited you about leading people to make that change? Why did you choose this example?

2. What do you most value about yourself as a leader? What are you willing to "go to the mat" for?

3. What do you experience as the core value of your college? Give some examples of how you experience those values.

4. If you had three wishes for your college, what would they be?

Team members then completed a Summary Sheet, using the following format:

1. What was the most appreciative quotable quote that came out of your interview?

2. What was the most compelling story that came out of your interview? What details and examples did the interviewee share? How were the interviewee and/or others changed by the story?

3. What was the most "life-giving" moment of the interview for you as a listener?

4. Did a particularly creative and/or innovative example of exemplary college leadership emerge during the interview? If so, describe what you learned about it.

5. What three themes stood out most for you during the interview?

Team members then took turns sharing each other's stories. As they discussed them, Dantino posted the life-giving forces they discovered in the stories and then helped the team *map* the positive core. The resulting list of what participants wanted more of included: caring attitude for students extended to all; listening deeply, more - and better; directness and honesty in college wide communication; creative thinking and flexibility; empowering people to succeed; clarifying expectations and accountability; recognition of exceptionally positive moments and people (best for all above self); develop better systems; and timely responses.

The team then used those themes or forces that gave life to Exemplary College Leadership at the College to develop a Provocative Proposition: "Asnuntuck Community College is deeply committed to the success of its students and employees through caring, direct and honest communications, and fosters an environment where creative thinking and flexibility are cultivated. People are empowered to succeed."

Once the shared image of a preferred future was created, the team members discussed ways of strategically acting on their intentions to bring the image to life on a daily basis. They agreed that several of the strategies could be acted on immediately by conducting additional one-on-one conversations or interviews with others with whom they did not ordinarily interact. They also agreed to hold follow-up sessions to track progress on the strategic actions and to address some of the Parking Lot issues.

To help the team members sustain the energy and ideas they generated during the Inquiry, Dantino said that she would be "sending them pictures as they engaged in the process as a motivator to keep moving because whether they realized it or not, they were actually having a good time in exploration."

As a result of the Inquiry, Danatino said that she "learned that the challenges faced by educational institutions are by and large human issues rather than procedural; that the simple courtesies of recognition, appreciation, and value are at the core of what people define as successful, productive places to work. My 'personal best' experience related to facilitating the Inquiry was in seeing and having a part in facilitating the subtle transformation that occurred with individuals who moved from adversarial to thoughtfully reflective to recognition during the process. "

> "... the members were hungry for guidance and affirmation of their purpose."

Jayne Peaslee, director of professional development at Corning Community College, New York, facilitated an Inquiry for administrators on the topic of shared governance which had recently been redesigned to allow all employees to have a voice in decision-making: Faculty Assembly, Administrators Assembly and Professional and Support Staff (PaSS) Assembly. Peaslee worked with the Administrators Assembly, 46 mid- managers and administrative assistants representing all non-academic departments of the College. She facilitated AI over a five-month period, immediately after regularly scheduled monthly meetings. Members of the Assembly wanted to use AI to create a mission statement that would inspire the group's actions.

The positive topic that the Core Group identified for Inquiry was Practices We Do Best and to use those best practices as a guide for creating more successes. Members of Administrators Assembly paired up and interviewed each other regarding a time when they felt most valued at the College. From themes that were present in the stories, the group created several Provocative Propositions. They also used the 'goose egg' technique (See next pages and Watkins & Mohr, 2003, p. 137-138) to identify the dreams and values of their ideal working conditions, as well as the design elements that supported those ideal working conditions.

The Assembly used the Provocative Propositions and the life-giving forces to create a mission statement: "The commitment of the Administrators Assembly of the College Association of Corning Community College is to establish an environment whereby members express their issues and ideas, discuss possibilities and initiate change. The members foster teamwork with colleagues and students through appreciation and respect. We are passionate about the success of students and address student needs proactively. As a vibrant leadership group that encourages full participation of our members, we celebrate the accomplishments of all."

They presented the mission statement to the College's Joint Council, which had member representation from all three assemblies and was chaired by the president of the College, for consensus approval. The College president planned to present the statement to the Board of Trustees and file it as an official mission statement for the Administrators Assembly.

Administrators Assembly's officers planned to incorporate a method of celebrating the accomplishments of members each month by presenting a trophy award to one person who is "a star above the rest" in exhibiting appreciation and respect to colleagues and sincerely addressing student needs.

Peaslee was the Administrator Assembly chair-elect for the following year; in that role, she planned to incorporate a time at each meeting to share "great happenings at CCC" where people share their success stories and also plan to have a monthly "a star above" award presentation to a deserving member who exhibits appreciation and respect to colleagues and students.

Peaslee said, "I learned from this experience that indeed the members were hungry for guidance and affirmation of their purpose. They need positive reinforcement and continual assurance that they do make a difference in the new governance structure."

Her 'personal best' experience was when the group composed a mission statement that was such a positive affirmation of who they were as members of the Administrators Assembly. They exclaimed, "Yes! This is our Mission Statement! This is who we are!" She said she could see the pride in their eyes and the satisfaction of being a part of a group that will move forward with integrity and respect for CCC employees and students.

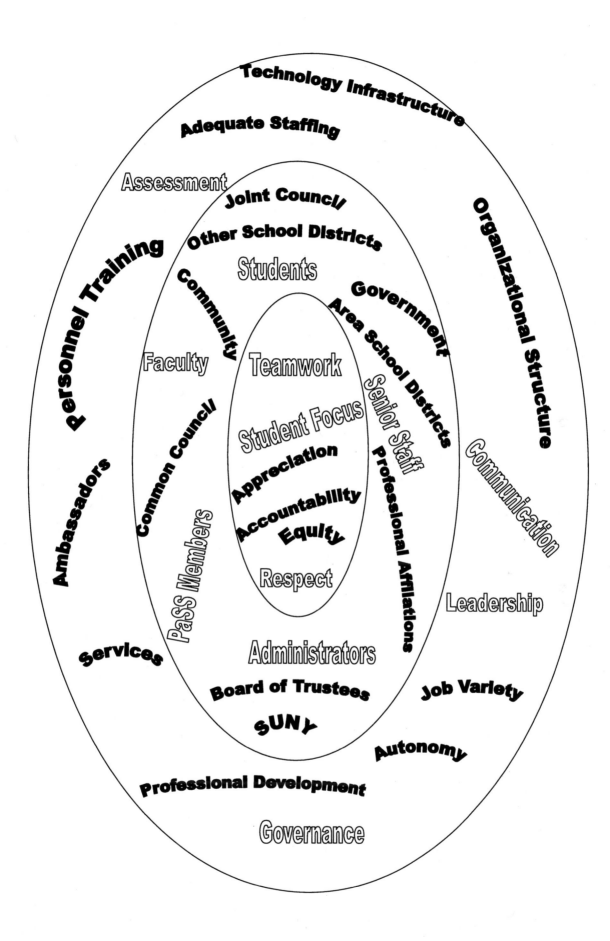

Andrea Ursuy and Betty Lopez, Delta College, Michigan, co-facilitated an inquiry with the Association of Delta College Office Professionals (ADCOP). ADCOP was a relatively new association for support staff at Delta College; it had 40 members. A voluntary organization, its mission is to promote professional development and provide opportunities for fellowship. Members of ADCOP join because they are committed to becoming "better at work" by utilizing professional development opportunities.

> **"My 'personal best' experience was working with one participant who thought that she was lacking in the 'success department' to help her realize that she had a long list of successes to choose from … Her level of participation increased when she began to realize the great things that she has done throughout the past year."**

Ursuy and Lopez co-facilitated a two-hour Inquiry for ADCOP into the topic of Planting a Positive Seed for Success. The purposes of the Inquiry were to: search for the root causes of personal and professional successes; help develop an appreciative mindset; and help understand what staff wanted more of in their lives.

ADCOP identified three main themes that stood out when they told their stories. Those themes were: valuing family; taking pride in accomplishments at home and at work; and the importance of planning for the future. From those themes, the group created a Provocative Proposition: "We take pride in our accomplishments, our future plans and especially our family."

They also created four Strategic Intentions: make good choices; pick your battles; take a fun class; and make a point to "make a good memory" at work, with family, etc.

Building on the Inquiry topic of Planting a Positive Seed for Success, the facilitators provided the participants with seed packets and chocolate – seeds to signify growth and chocolate for energy to continue the positive as a way of being.

Lopez said that her 'personal best' was the positive interaction she experienced with the participants and the fact that they were pleased with the outcomes that resulted from the AI process.

Ursuy said, "I learned that facilitating an Inquiry helped me to understand the AI process at a deeper level. I was also more confident in facilitating the Inquiry than I had anticipated I would be. My 'personal best' experience was working with one participant who thought that she was lacking in the 'success department' to help her realize that she had a long list of successes to choose from, including her relationship with her daughter and a project that she recently completed at work. Her level of participation increased when she began to realize the great things that she has done throughout the past year."

## South Piedmont Community College, NC

> **" … to see those 'rolling eyes' becoming engaged in the process and participating was a very positive experience."**

Sharon Grooms, director of teacher education, and Stuart Wasilowski, dean of workforce development, both at South Piedmont Community College in North Carolina, co-facilitated an Inquiry with the six members of the College's Senior Leadership Team (SLT) on the topic of Meetings that Work!

The SLT created a Provocative Proposition: "Meetings at SPCC have a purpose, agenda, operational procedures (minutes/documentation); meetings are focused, where participants are empowered; meetings start and stop on time, and make progress toward a goal."

Their Strategic Intentions were: provide staff with additional training on how to make meetings that work; track/measure feedback on meeting success; and implement the meeting standard in meetings going forward.

Grooms and Wasilowski were invested in the organization and the process. They saw that changes occurred as a result of the Inquiry. Agendas changed and a bold statement was imprinted on the VP's agenda as a reminder to all of how they will make meetings that work.

Grooms and Wasilowski intended to follow-up with the members of the SLT to see just how they had changed the way they operated in their meetings. As the meeting agenda and minutes are made public, they should be able to see a change in the outcomes and meeting substance.

Celebrating successes would be subtle as the co-facilitators acted in a supportive and consultative role. As they worked closely with the participants, they could support and celebrate the changes as they reviewed their meeting experiences over time.

The facilitators said, "The wish/hope for the inquiry was two-fold. First, was to inform the institutional leadership of the AI process. Secondly, was to give the participants something more substantive than a report back on the AI experience and provide an experience that could impact the organization overall."

They learned, "Much was gained by working thru the process and then to be queried afterwards about AI. The experience tested the AI process for the facilitators. We saw firsthand how to move through the process. We experienced the 'rolled eyes' of participants and the full engagement of others. It was important to have two facilitators in the room to keep the energy, recording, conversation and questions flowing. It was good to have provided the questions in advance so that participants came prepared to participate." (NOTE: Typically, the Interview Guide is not distributed in advance of a face-to-face session). "The expectation of participation was set in advance."

Grooms and Wasilowski agreed that, "There were a number of positive moments within the process. The best moment of the process was the quick development of the Provocative Proposition. The group seemed to rally around the statement quickly and had built enthusiasm to move toward that statement. Secondly, to see those 'rolling eyes' becoming engaged in the process and participating was a very positive experience. Finally, to have the overall experience to work through the process, with a challenge that was not wholly the problem of the facilitators, was good. To have that objectivity was a great experience. This opportunity has given the facilitators the confidence to take this on in other areas within the institution."

## Chapter Seven

## SELF STUDY FOR ACCREDITATION

### Accreditation of Two-Year Institutions

> "What continues to catch and inspire me is how the power of conversations translates into real action and real differences, revealing again and again the creativity and innovation of our community colleges."

The United States has six regional associations and seven commissions that accredit community colleges and/or technical/career institutions. Strong incentives exist for institutions to become voluntary members of these associations, and become and remain accredited by their regional commission. These incentives include the fact that the public generally believes that accredited institutions are of higher quality than non-accredited institutions. Also, from a very practical standpoint, students that attend accredited institutions are eligible to receive Higher Education Act, Title IV federal funds to help fund their postsecondary education; students attending unaccredited institutions are not. Unaccredited institutions usually are not eligible to receive state appropriations or state and federal grants.

The six regional associations and seven commissions are: Middle States Association of Colleges and Schools/Middle States Commission on Higher Education (MSCHE); New England Association of Schools and Colleges/Commission on Institutions of Higher Education (NEASC-CIHE); New England Association of Schools and Colleges/Commission on Technical and Career Institutions (NEASE-CTCI); North Central Association of Colleges and Schools/The Higher Learning Commission (NCA/HLC); Northwest Commission on Colleges and Universities (NWCCU); Southern Association of Colleges and Schools/Commission on Colleges (SACS); and Western Association of Schools and Colleges/Accrediting Commission for Community and Junior Colleges (WASC/AACCJ).

Each regional association/commission operates independently from the other regional associations/commissions; however, the Council for Higher Education Accreditation (CHEA) oversees them all. While institutional membership is voluntary, all of the commissions require member institutions to undergo a periodic self-study, an appraisal of itself in terms of the commission's standards in accord with the institution's stated purposes, in order to acquire or retain accreditation.

### Appreciative Inquiry and Self Study for Accreditation

At least three of the six regional accrediting commissions appear to allow, encourage or require Appreciative Inquiry (AI), or processes similar to AI, as part of an institution's self-study process: North Central Association of Colleges and Schools/The Higher Learning Commission (NCA/HLC); Western Association of Schools and Colleges/Accrediting Commission for Community and Junior Colleges; and Northwest Commission on Colleges and Universities (NWCCU). The author did not investigate the policies of the other three commissions.

One of the commissions, NCA/HLC, encourages the use of what it calls Vital Focus Conversations as part of an institution's self-study process; the process uses AI as its conceptual framework (2004). Vital Focus Conversations was developed by Lynn Priddy, director of education and training for HLC. Another commission, WASC/ACCJC, requires institutions to use On-Going Self-Reflective Dialogue, which is in direct alignment with AI (2002). And a third commission, NWCCU, allows "a variety of approaches to self-study . . . An institution is free to propose some variation in the design of the self-study which it considers to be of intrinsic value as long as the overarching purposes of a comprehensive self-study are met and all Commission accreditation criteria are addressed" (2003).

AI research, theory and practice suggest that AI can be used by any organization to discover its strengths and successes, and create more of those strengths and successes by: (1) telling and sharing stories about times when things were going really well around the institution (i.e., uncovering its own best experiences and practices) that relate to accreditation standards or other topics important to student and organizational learning; (2) collaboratively inquiring into the conditions that were present in those exceptional moments; (3) grounded in those past and present best-practice stories, collaboratively creating visions of the institution's future that will support more of those exceptional moments; and (4) being inspired to make changes in organizational culture, processes and structures that will allow more of those conditions to prevail.

Rather than taking the traditional linear, cause-and-effect approach to incremental change, AI can bring about transformational change, even in academic institutions where people have been trained to see the world through a hypercritical lens. As two highly experienced AI practitioners proclaim and have experienced, AI can bring about organizational change "at the speed of imagination" (Watkins & Mohr, 2001). One reason for this is that people are less resistant to change when they are both fully involved in and empowered by the change effort. Another reason is that when people collaboratively create positive images of the future, they will take positive actions in the present to move toward that image.

## Examples of How AI Has Been Used in Self Study for Accreditation

Community colleges have used AI for Vital Focus Conversations, On-Going Self-Reflective Dialogue and Variation in the Design of a Self Study.

*Vital Focus Conversations*

NCA/HLC began encouraging institutions to use an alternative approach to the self-study process through its Academic Quality Improvement Program (AQIP) that was formed in 1999 with funding from the Pew Charitable Trusts. As previously mentioned, AQIP uses AI as the conceptual framework for a component of the self-study process: Vital Focus Conversations. According to Priddy, more than 50 institutions have used Vital Focus Conversations as part of their self studies since 1999 (Priddy, 2005).

An institution in the NCA/HLC region that was preparing to use AQIP's alternative approach to self study made some of its hard-copy materials available to the author so that she could understand and describe the model (2004). According to those materials, Vital Focus Conversations: Committing to Conversation, Acting on What Matters, is a series of three institution-wide conversations that parallel the five generic processes of AI (also known as the 4 or 5-Ds). The Vital Focus Conversations are preceded by something called a Constellation Survey, an institution-wide survey; the results of the survey are used to inform the three conversations. Usually, someone from AQIP facilitates the conversations and oversees the survey.

AQIP proposes seven ground rules for the facilitated conversations: (1) All ideas are valid; (2) Listening is as important as speaking; (3) Plans and discussions are confidential; (4) Time frames will be observed; (5) All questions are important; (6) New ideas are welcome; and (7) We'll have fun.

*Conversation One.* The college community comes together and, in small groups called table groups, holds a series of structured conversations. In Conversation One, first individuals, then pairs and finally small groups, discover what it is that they collectively agree is of greatest importance - what matters most - at their college. They use a series of appreciative questions to discover their best experiences at the college, something they connect to on a deep and personal level.

87

Specifically, each individual is asked to think about a peak experience they have had at the college - a time when they felt really engaged in and excited about their work - when both they and the college seemed to be operating at peak performance.

Then two individuals pair up and interview each other, asking these questions: "What is your peak experience or 'high point?' What things do you value most about your work? About the college? What are the core factors that give life and vitality to the college - those things that draw you to and keep you there?"

The pairs are then invited to share each other's stories with their small group. "In your table group, briefly summarize (do not retell - take only two to three minutes) the notes from your interviews. After listening to the stories/notes, discuss the common themes in your peak experiences." The group then discusses and agrees on three or four of the most important themes they heard in the peak experiences - characteristics, ways of working - that matter most. They then compare their group conclusions to the results of Part 1 of the Constellation Survey, which is a way of bringing additional voices into the room.

Finally, each small group discusses and agrees on one process that they believe is most important for focus and one high-performance principle that is most important to develop. Each small group then posts these most important processes and high-performance principles on a What Matters Most wall.

*Conversation Two.* In Conversation Two, first individuals, then the large group and, finally, small groups are asked to focus on answers to this question: "What do you agree are core strengths or vibrant aspects of this college and its culture?" This question also is very similar to one that is typically used in AI.

To prepare for the discussion, each individual is asked to "Jot down your endings to these statements: (a) Two real strengths about my college that I've noticed are . . . and (b) A process (advising, recruiting, new program development, budgeting) that really works well right now is . . ."

The large group then discusses: "What is a specific example of a recent change that has resulted in this college being more student-focused or student-centered? Where is collaboration thriving at this college (internal, external, among departments, etc.)? What have students told you are your strengths? Employers? What do you see as the core strengths (specific) of your faculty? Support staff? Administrators?"

The small groups then review Part 2 of Constellation Results and, again, bringing additional voices into the room, discuss and agree on one strength the group agrees is a highlight, defining quality or best practice at the college.

*Conversation Three.* Conversation Three invites the college community to discuss this question, "What do you most wish for the college? What, if accomplished, would make a significant difference?"

First, individuals are asked to answer this question for themselves: "If you could make three recommendations for action at your college that would make a significant difference, what would these be?" In AI, this is known as the Three Wishes question. The large group then reviews the results of Part 3 from the Constellation Survey. Then individuals voluntarily form new small groups around the topic they are most interested in. Before more discussion, each individual first completes an Idea Analysis Form for his or her three recommendations, or wishes.

After everyone completes the Form, each person takes turn sharing her/his recommendation and its critical aspects and differences to be made. The small group then brainstorms and records common themes across the recommendations, critical aspects and desired results or differences to be made. Small-group members then discuss and agree on the common ideas across the recommendations. Together, they use those themes to collaboratively create a statement, known in AI as a Provocative Proposition, that describes what the small group most wants to create for the college's future. Here are the "stretch" directions: "Take time to dream in the most ideal terms of what really would make a difference at the college and to the students and others it serves. Really stretch your thinking, be creative, think big, think beyond today" (2004).

Provocative Propositions, sometimes called Vision, Dream or Possibility Statements, as they are described in the Vital Focus Conversations literature, are somewhat different from those described in the AI literature. In Vital Focus Conversations, they take the form and language of recommendations and reasons for the recommendations. Here's an example:

We *recommend* that the college commit the financial and human resources to establish itself as the preferred provider throughout the Midwest of premier on-line adult literacy and college prep/developmental courses and services...*Because* we have concluded that in the highly competitive online learning world, there will be two types of participants, those who originate the courses and those who use the courses. The college has the mission and intellectual resources as well as the competitive drive to be creative originators of top-quality learning opportunities for those who most need basic skills and knowledge and learning aptitudes, as well as technological abilities (2004).

The form and language of a Provocative Proposition resulting from a "classic" AI would take the same essential content and use present-tense verbs and language. Using the same ideas as the "recommend/because" example above, here's how it might read:

At this college, we are the preferred provider throughout the Midwest of premier on-line adult literacy and college prep/developmental courses and services. We have the mission and intellectual resources as well as the competitive drive to be creative originators of top-quality learning opportunities for those who most need basic skills and knowledge and learning aptitudes, as well as technological abilities.

According to the research and theory of AI, using present tense language, as if the Provocative Proposition were already happening all of the time rather than just in exceptional past or present moments, makes the vision, dream or possibility more compelling to the people in the organization or group. The idea is that, in fact, it *is* already happening, in the exceptional moments that people shared in their Conversations.

Each small group then presents its Provocative Proposition to the large group as recommendations for action. Here's another place where the Vital Focus Conversations differ somewhat from "classic" AI. In AI, participants in the process would then, as a small or large group, collaboratively create specific Strategic Initiatives (also called Strategic Intentions, Pilot Projects, or Bold Ideas) to begin realizing their Provocative Proposition. Also, each individual might be invited to make a Commitment, Offer, or Request to the small and/or large group to begin realizing the Provocative Proposition. These inspired actions would then move forward without needing additional approvals; the approvals would have been granted during the Inquiry, rather than after.

Additionally, before leaving the session, the AI facilitator(s) might ask for one volunteer from each small group to form a team that would later synthesize all of the micro Provocative Propositions into a macro Provocative Proposition for the college and send it out to the college community as a draft for written feedback and perhaps for further dialogue. The AI Facilitator(s) also might ask for volunteers to form a team that would help the college notice and celebrate each and every story of success, stories of the college's movement toward the Provocative Propositions and Strategic Initiatives. These stories of success become a way of monitoring progress and outcomes, including any new and improvised initiatives that might spring up. The stories also generate positive energy for on-going movement and dialogue. Over time, the Inquiries result in measurable outcomes, impact and results.

The Community College of Denver (CCD) participated in the Academic Quality Improvement Program (AQIP) through the Higher Learning Commission, a member of the North Central Association of Colleges and Schools. A. Allen Butcher, Coordinator of Online Learning, and Darlene Nold, Executive Director of Institutional Research, shared the story of how CCD used AQIP's nine categories for measuring quality of service at the College as the positive topics for Appreciative Inquiry and self study. A team of eight employees from Community College of Denver attended a four-day Appreciative Inquiry Facilitator Training (AIFT©) in June 2004. The team went back to the College and used the techniques learned from AI as the process for its upcoming self study for accreditation.

> "... the Appreciative Inquiry process proved to be a valuable one for bringing all constituencies of the College together, getting everyone focused on a specific initiative."

At the College's Fall 2004 Convocation, 183 employees came together to begin the self-study process. Everyone was sorted into three rooms and, upon entering the room, they self-selected into one of nine topics, sitting with others who selected the same topic. The employees at each table then paired up and shared "Best Experience" stories in response to an unconditionally positive question about their particular topic. Each topic ended up with three tables of people, one from each room, inquiring into the topic, for a total of 27 small groups.

Here are the nine topics and questions:
1. Helping students learn: "What was your best experience helping students learn?"
2. Accomplishing other distinctive objectives: "What was the best experience you had accomplishing something unique or distinctive?"
3. Understanding students and other stakeholder needs: "How have we best understood student and community needs? What was your best experience in understanding (empathizing with) the needs of others?"
4. Valuing people: "What was your best experience where you felt valued or you helped others to feel valued?"
5. Leading and communicating: "What was your best experience where you experienced good leadership through effective communication? Describe an event in which you provided good leadership through effective communication."
6. Supporting institutional operations: "What was your best experience helping the institution run well?"
7. Measuring effectiveness: "Talk about your best experience when you knew what you were doing was working."
8. Planning continuous improvement: "How do you keep focused on getting better and better? What is your best experience in continually improving something?"
9. Building collaborative relationships: "What were your best experiences building collaborative relationships?"

Following the paired interviews, the individuals at each table shared the highlights of their partners' stories. Then each table group identified a high-energy theme from the stories which they reported out to the entire room. In the end, 27 high-energy themes were identified, three themes – known as life-giving forces - for each of the AQIP categories: *When _____ was at its best at Community College of Denver, here's what gave it life.* Following Convocation, 107 faculty and staff conducted ongoing meetings to further the inquiries into the nine topics; this occurred throughout the Fall 2004 semester.

Each topic group began to further examine what CCD would look like if it were experiencing more of these exceptional moments, more or all of the time. The groups first created a visual image of what the College would look like, using mixed-media art, a song, or skit. They presented their visual images to the entire group. Using the metaphor they created as a springboard, they then developed a Provocative Proposition, or word image, to stimulate awareness, provide guidance and provoke actions. What would it "look like" or "sound like" if people at CCD were experiencing their exceptional moments more or all of the time?

To realize the Provocative Propositions, or visions, people were invited to develop action items to help them realize their Dreams. Based on what people learned in the Inquiry, the major outcome was a strategic initiative to improve institutional communication, both formally and informally. Their 27 action items were grouped into seven action areas:

(1) Create opportunities for informal communication (4 action items)

(2) Create opportunities to enhance formal communication - sharing with institutional leaders (6 action items)

(3) Collaborate and communicate about/with stakeholders (4 action items)

(4) Provide training for professional development (1 action item)

(5) Refocus on teaching and learning - Student needs / Student focus (5 action items)

(6) Create a climate of trust through open lines of communication (4 action items)

(7) Revise institutional planning and project management process (3 action items)

One of the primary deliverables for the AQIP accreditation process is a System Portfolio, typically a hundred-page response to the AQIP category questions that address methods for improving key systems toward enabling higher performance. In Spring 2005, CCD administration and the AI Facilitation Team planned the process of creating CCD's AQIP System Portfolio. Volunteers were solicited to comprise AQIP Explorer Teams for researching and writing reports in answer to the AQIP Category questions.

Each Exploration Team was comprised of one or two people who had been trained to be AI Facilitators, with an average of six other volunteers. They spent late spring and all summer researching and writing their reports, interviewing people in and outside the College for needed information. Then they used the AI-inspired Provocative Propositions and action items for the Improvements section of the System Portfolio.

Beginning in Fall 2005, the staff of the CCD Institutional Advancement office served as editors, pulling together all of the Explorer Teams' individual sections, making sure that CCD's AQIP System Portfolio spoke in a single coherent voice. CCD executive staff had final input to the content submitted for the Academic Quality Improvement Program report. The System Portfolio was submitted to the Higher Learning Commission in November of 2005.

According to Nold, the Appreciative Inquiry process proved to be a valuable one for bringing all constituencies of the College together, getting everyone focused on a specific initiative, in addition to getting the Systems Portfolio written. CCD's portfolio was reviewed by HCL; feedback was received in Spring 2006 indicating the College's strengths and opportunities for improvement. Many of the action steps within the strategic initiative of improving institutional communication were implemented. According to Nold, as of Fall 2007, employees continue to take inspired actions to strengthen communication at CCD.

*On-Going, Self-Reflective Dialogue*

As mentioned earlier, WASC/ACCJC requires institutions to participate in what they call On-Going Self-Reflective Dialogue. As described in the ACCJC literature, AI is a process that could be used for the Dialogue.

In an introduction to *Accreditation Standards* (2002), ACCJC described what it meant by ongoing, self-reflective dialogue:

"An effective institution maintains an ongoing, self-reflective dialogue about its quality and improvement."

"An institution-wide dialogue must be at the heart of the self-evaluation process for the college community to gain a comprehensive perspective of the institution."

"A college-wide dialogue that integrates the elements of the Standards provides the complete view of the institution that is needed to verify integrity and to promote quality and improvement."

Dialogue is defined in a glossary as "self-reflective exchanges engaged in by the college community, characterized by a free exchange of ideas without the purpose of defending or deciding on a course of action."

In another document, *Guide to Evaluating Institutions* (2004), ACCJC describes On-Going, Self-Reflective Dialogue in more detail:

"A dialogue is a group discussion among 'colleagues,' often facilitated, that is designed to explore complex issues, create greater group intelligence and facilitate group learning. The idea of 'colleagues' is important; dialogue occurs where individuals see themselves as colleagues. In order for the group to engage in dialogue, individuals must suspend their own views to listen fully to one another in order to understand each other's viewpoints. Groups engaged in dialogue develop greater insights, shared meanings and ultimately, collective understanding of complex issues and how best to address them.

"Dialogue improves *collective* thinking. A practice of dialogue can have benefits for the individual as well as the institution. Dialogue can help build self-awareness, improve communication skills, strengthen teams and stimulate innovation that fosters effective change. Dialogues are powerful, transformational experiences that lead to both personal and collaborative action. But dialogic discussions also allow controversial topics that may have in the past become sources of disagreement and division to be explored in a more useful context that can lead to greater group insight."

In "classic" AI sessions, AI Facilitators encourage the organizational members to see each other as colleagues, regardless of rank in the room - from president to custodian.

ACCJC suggests ground rules for Dialogue: (1) Listening actively; (2) Seeking to understand; (3) Giving everyone the opportunity to talk; and (4) Trying not to interrupt. ACCJC also suggests retaining a facilitator to "ensure that the ground rules are maintained" and to "help clarify themes and ideas."

## San Bernardino Valley College, CA

> " . . . positive change can take place - when the change comes from the participants and the core values they possess."

AI is one approach an institution might use to facilitate On-Going, Self-Reflective Dialogue. Many institutions are using AI for on-going, self-reflective dialogue on topics that focus on issues of critical importance to institutions, e.g., student learning and student success. San Bernardino Valley College (SBVC) in California used AI to become a more learning-centered institution (Weiss, 2004).

At San Bernardino Community College District, after a fall in-service session that focused on the concept of The Learning College, Donald Averill, District Chancellor, encouraged the colleges - Crafton Hills College and SBVC - to share with him what they were doing to become learning colleges. As on many community college campuses, immediate resistance came up because most faculty and others believed that they already were learning colleges. And, of course, to some extent they were; Averill wanted them to become even more so.

Denise Whittaker, SBVC president, and the college council asked Kay Weiss, coordinator of professional and organizational development at SBVC, to think of ways she could help the College become more learning centered, without encountering the usual resistance. A certified AI Facilitator, Weiss proposed to facilitate an Inquiry for the College community on the topic of A Model Learning-Centered College. Working with a Core Group made up of a student, two faculty members, two classified employees and a manager, Weiss helped the team plan and lead the facilitation of five AI Summits on that topic. The

Summits involved a total of 125 faculty, staff, managers and students; they were held in the morning, afternoon and evening in order to get the broadest participation.

It is worth noting that ACCJC/WASC, in its Self-Study Manual, encourages colleges to "provide evidence of broad participation and a commitment to making a concerted effort to providing the opportunity for all voices to be heard in the self-study effort" (2004).

Rather than the traditional focus on closing the gaps, or solving the problems, or telling the college community what others believed a learning college was, AI helped participants engage in a structured dialogue in which they studied, or inquired into, the conditions that fostered their own best learning-centered experiences at SBVC. Then, using those best-experience stories, participants created Provocative Propositions of what SBVC would look like if it were being a learning-centered college all or more of the time, rather than just in the exceptional moments they discovered in the interviews and ensuing dialogue.

Here's one example of a Provocative Proposition the participants at one of the five Summits created: "SBVC accepts the responsibility of providing a quality inquiry-based learning environment that supports all learning styles and promotes real world application and life-long learning" (Weiss, 2004).

The Summit participants then created Pilot Projects to move SBVC toward their Provocative Propositions: (1) Senate leadership in establishing college-wide student learning outcomes and assessment processes (now required by ACCJC); (2) development of an on-line college; and (3) information kiosks at peak registration times. People then voluntarily formed teams to work on these Pilot Projects, regardless of job description. According to both Whittaker and Weiss, these teams moved forward on the Pilot Projects.

What participants discovered was that they could create a vision of what a learning college would look like based on their own high-point learning experiences. They also could create inspired actions for realizing the vision.

Weiss said, "An overwhelming number of participants identified the process as an incredibly positive one - and valued the opportunity to share successes, to brainstorm solutions and to work on ways to 'live our mission.' . . . The core team developed plans and timelines to assure the campus that positive change can take place - when the change comes from the participants and the core values they possess."

The College's Council then requested that SBVC use AI to develop its strategic plan. See chapter three for detailed stories about using AI for strategic planning.

*Variation in the Design of a Self Study*

As mentioned earlier, NWCCU allows colleges to vary the design of a self study as long as the overarching purposes of a comprehensive self study are met and all Commission accreditation criteria are addressed.

Clackamas Community College, OR

"AI has helped us really know each other, and that creates unforeseen positive results every day."

According to Rich Henry, an independent consultant in Washington State, Clackamas Community College (CCC) in Oregon used AI as part of its self-study for accreditation. In February 2005, Henry told the Clackamas story in an Instructional Leadership Abstract published by the National Council of Instructional Administrators (Henry, 2005). NCIA is one of 23 affiliate councils of the American Association of Community Colleges. With permission from NCIA and Henry, here is CCC's slightly-edited story.

CCC identified four goals for its accreditation process: (1) receive 10-year affirmation of accreditation; (2) engage 100 percent of the campus community; (3) use the accreditation steering committee as a model for the campus on how to be a learning community, using technology and AI techniques; and (4) use the self study to tell the Clackamas story and be proud of who it was.

CCC fully embraced the self-study as a framework that provided additional focus to what they were already doing on a continual basis. In the words of Dian Connett, dean of instructional services, "Accreditation is planning and planning is accreditation." In fact, as part of its last self study, CCC adapted its division and department annual planning practices and templates so that their collected documentation comprises most of their self-study data collection. Connett pointed out, "We've changed the ways we do our daily and yearly work so that they demonstrate the accreditation standards."

One of the fundamental components of AI is the Appreciative Interview. No matter what the scale of an Inquiry, involving a few people or thousands, it usually begins with a one-on-one paired interview, using carefully crafted unconditionally positive questions to discover life-giving moments and conditions, factors and forces in the human system under study that supported success or a peak experience. The interview not only gathers and creates new information, it also invariably creates a bond between interview partners.

Donna Acord, associate dean for extended studies, said that, for her, the best part of the self study at CCC was the opportunity to meet and work with different people across the campus. These new relationships, deepened by the AI approach, benefited the self study and far beyond. "AI has helped us really know each other and that creates unforeseen positive results every day."

AI is especially effective at generating and amplifying what Henry calls "virtuous circles" (rather than vicious cycles) by specifically focusing attention on times and circumstances when the organization and the people were at their best. AI research and theory suggest that, in human systems, what we focus on increases. If we focus on problems, they will increase; if we focus on successes, they will increase. Clackamas Community College leveraged this effect in its self study. Connett said, "We love it here. It's all about the people."

## Summary

Many community colleges have plugged into the power of AI to invigorate their self studies for accreditation or other organizational self-assessment processes. Among them were Community College of Denver in Colorado, San Bernardino Valley College in California and Clackamas Community College in Oregon. According to Priddy, others included Phillips Community College in Arkansas, Lamar Community College in Colorado, Lake Superior College and Hennepin Technical College in Minnesota, and Madison Area Technical College in Wisconsin.

Priddy said, "Compelling questions - the chance to put on the table the most important conversations - bring people together to discern what matters most to do now to make a significant difference. Through the use of AI, many community colleges have reframed self study around such questions, entering into new conversations that shift accreditation from a matter of compliance into a matter of commitment to and shared responsibility for student learning, educational excellence and institutional integrity. What continues to catch and inspire me is how the power of conversations translates into real action and real differences, revealing again and again the creativity and innovation of our community colleges."

References for Chapter Seven

Accrediting Commission References Taken From:

North Central Association of Colleges and Schools/The Higher Learning Commission (NCA/HLC)
    Documents:
    *Committing to Conversations, Acting on What Matters.* Faxed copy dated November 23, 2004.
    Academic Quality Improvement Program (AQIP).
    *Understanding AQIP*, AQIP, 2003.
    www. aqip.org

Northwest Commission on Colleges and Universities (NWCCU) Documents:
    *Accreditation Handbook*, 2003.
    www.nwccu.org

Western Association of Schools and Colleges/Accrediting Commission for Community and Junior Colleges
    (WASC/ACCJC) Documents:
    *Accreditation Standards*, June 2002.
    *Guide to Evaluating Institutions*, August 2004.
    *Self-Study Manual*, 2004.
    www.accjc.org

Other References:

Henry, R. (2005). Discovering and growing what gives life: appreciative inquiry in community colleges.
    *Instructional Leadership Abstracts*, Lubbock, TX: Texas Tech University.

Priddy, L. (2005-2007). Personal communications by email and phone.

Watkins, J. M. & B. J. Mohr (2001). *Appreciative Inquiry: Change at the Speed of Imagination.* San
    Francisco: Jossey-Bass/Pfeiffer.

Weiss, K. (2004). *Practicum Report for Certification as an AI Facilitator.* San Bernardino, CA: Author.

# Chapter Eight

## MORE STORIES OF POSITIVE CHANGE

Community college leaders and consultants shared stories about a number of Inquiries they facilitated at eight community colleges and at a national conference. The Inquiries focused on assessing organizational strengths, celebrating successes, organizational culture, student engagement, student recruitment and retention, and teaching and learning. Sites of the Inquiries were: Bakersfield College and Rio Hondo College in California; Edison Community College and Southern State College in Ohio; Houston Community College in Texas; Oakland Community College in Michigan; St. Louis Community College in Missouri; Southside Virginia Community College in Virginia; and the Teaching for a Change conference in Colorado.

*Assessing Organizational Strengths*

### Oakland Community College, MI

> **"I was able to hit the ground running at Oakland Community College and quickly help the College begin to build on its strengths and successes."**

When Mary Spangler became chancellor at Oakland Community College (OCC), she wanted to know what people believed were the strengths of the College so that she could help the College community build on those strengths. At the very beginning of her time at Oakland, she interviewed a number of faculty, administrators and support staff, using the following Appreciative Interview Guide. Spangler later left Oakland to become chancellor of Houston Community College in Texas.

### Background

As the new Chancellor at OCC, I believe that my primary responsibility is to help OCC continue to move forward in a positive direction. In order to fulfill that responsibility, I will need your help and the help of the other people at OCC. Toward that end, I need to get to know you, your strengths, and the strengths of the other people at OCC. I also need to get to know the strengths of the college as a whole. One way for me to uncover the primary strengths of OCC is to have you and others tell me about your own best past and current experiences at OCC. I've developed four questions that will help me uncover those strengths. We can spend an average of xx minutes on each question. When I have synthesized the patterns from this and other interviews, I will report the results holistically to the college community.

1. Tell me a story about the best experience you've had with OCC. When did you feel most alive, most involved, most excited about your involvement? What made it an exciting experience? Who was involved? Describe the event.

2. What are the things you value most deeply about:

a. Yourself?

b. Your work?

c. OCC?

d. What is the single most important thing that OCC has contributed to your life?

3. What do you experience as the core value or values of OCC? Give me some examples of how you experience those values.

4. What three wishes would you make to heighten the vitality and health of OCC?

Thank you for telling me your stories. As we move forward together, I will encourage us all to keep sharing our best experiences with each other so that we can build on our strengths to create even more successes.

In addition to the face-to-face interviews, Spangler then sent out an email to the entire College community.

Dear OCC Family,

It has been only ten short days since I invited your input in three separate areas: your best experience at OCC, the core values you observe in action, and two wishes to strengthen the college. I have been very pleased with the thoughtful and detailed responses to those questions. To date, I have received more than 50, printed each one, read the comments with great interest, and made notes on emerging themes and ideas. I want you to know your comments are important and helpful.

The purpose of this email is to encourage those of you who have not responded to take some time to give me your best thinking. That input will be reflected in the objectives the Chancellor's Council is developing to achieve the college's seven goals. It will also help to inform and shape the vision statement that will accompany the goals and objectives. To ensure your input is considered, please respond as soon as possible. The draft objectives will be distributed at the beginning of October for college-wide prioritizing.

I've included the three questions below for your convenience. Thank you in advance for your participation.

1. Describe the best experience you've had at OCC. When did you feel most involved and most excited about your involvement? What made it an exciting experience?

2. What do you experience as a core value of OCC? Can you give an example of how you experience the value?

3. What two wishes would you make to heighten the vitality and health of OCC?

Spangler said that, because of this appreciative assessment, "I was able to hit the ground running at Oakland Community College and quickly help the College begin to build on its strengths and successes." It also alerted the College community to Spangler's philosophy and personal style.

*Celebrating Successes*

Rio Hondo College, CA

A seven-person team from Rio Hondo College in California - Christine Aldrich, Cathy Butler, Gail Chabran, Suzanne Frederickson, Katie O'Brien, Gil Puga and Rene Tai participated in a statewide Appreciative Inquiry Facilitator Training (AIFT©) for California community colleges that was sponsored by the Professional Development Institute for Economic and Workforce Development. While the team didn't submit an official report to become certified as AI Facilitators, they informally reported that they had co-facilitated three campus introductory sessions about the AI philosophy and practice. The first was targeted toward managers and the second and third were open to and attended by faculty, staff and administration.

The team also borrowed an idea they picked up at the AIFT from Judy Walters, former vice chancellor at Peralta Community Colleges in California, who was also at the training. She, in turn, had picked up the idea from a video used in the AIFT, Celebrate What's Right With the World. The Rio Hondo team, in order to introduce the concepts and power of Appreciative Inquiry, created a video of What's Right with Rio. During the fall semester, the team worked with a campus film maker to document stories about what was working and what was positive about the College. The 10-minute video made its debut at the beginning of the winter semester; it was a great hit. The Board of Trustees also viewed the video and thoroughly enjoyed it. The video offered a humorous and touching testament to the possibilities of what Rio already was doing well, as well as outlining the potential of what Rio could be building on through Appreciative Inquiry.

## St. Louis Community College, MO

Donna Nelson (formerly Spaulding), coordinator of the Center for Teaching and Learning, at St. Louis Community College at Florissant Valley shared the following story. "We were in a summer meeting, brainstorming about how to create a positive, upbeat atmosphere for our August Opening Week events. This was not an easy task because our state budget had been cut several times last year and we were anticipating the same thing would happen again this year. But our president encouraged us to focus on what we could do, not on what we couldn't. When she said that, it led me directly to a thought of using AI stories.

> " . . . what might have been a downer week became an upbeat event because of the AI philosophy of telling good stories and getting people to focus on the positive in a situation."

"Several months before, some huge boulders had 'appeared' at various locations around campus, seemingly overnight. So I said, 'I'd like to hear the story of the rocks.' People in the meeting looked at me as if I'd lost my mind. But I knew there was a good story about the rocks. I wanted to hear the whole story and figured others might want to hear it, too. Discussing the possibilities of including the rock story in Opening Week led us to other uses of the word 'rock.' Rock music, rock candy, pet rocks – you get the idea.

"So, instead of returning to campus in August bemoaning the fact that there aren't enough classrooms and no money, Opening Week was entitled 'FV Rocks!' and our focus was on good stories. Our geology professor (quite a character) told the story of talking to the workers who were blasting the rocks to build a new highway and convincing them to let him have some of the big boulders. He also told us that 200 million years ago our campus was underwater as part of a prehistoric river and the boulders were part of an ancient reef that was being created then. Our president wove the FV Rocks theme into her presentation and helped us focus on the positive from both the past and for the future of our campus.

"On Friday of Opening Week we had our annual campus picnic. The culmination of the picnic was a Frisbee throwing contest. We provided the Frisbees that had FV Rocks! imprinted on them. Guess what the prizes were? You got it – sticks of rock candy!!

"People had fun. People told more good stories. And what might have been a downer week became an upbeat event because of the AI philosophy of telling good stories and getting people to focus on the positive in a situation."

## Bakersfield College, CA

Beverly Parsons, chief executive officer of InSites, and Clark Parsons, instructional technology specialist at Bakersfield College in California, co-facilitated an Inquiry at Bakersfield College (BC) that was part of a research project being conducted by InSites through a National Science Foundation grant. BC was the main pilot site for the grant.

> **"I really feel if more staff would participate, we would become a community working together again!"**

According to the co-facilitators, "The AI session we facilitated was a pilot test within the research study to determine if and how to use AI more broadly on campus. Given various political issues, it was determined best to pilot test the process with a small volunteer cross-role group. The participants in the AI session were a mix of faculty, students, staff and administrators at BC."

The co-facilitators used the Coordinating Committee at BC for the NSF grant as the Core Group. The BC Assessment Committee and the BC president were also involved. The positive topic of Inquiry was Student Success Through A Supportive College Culture.

At the AI session, small groups identified the life-giving forces (conditions, factors and forces in the system) that participants discovered were the ones that most supported Student Success Through A Supportive College Culture. The small groups then developed Provocative Propositions, two of which were: "Active Participation Empowers: Go APE" ; and "We maintain a supportive environment where people are willing to try new things to improve student success." The groups also developed three Strategic Intentions: community building, effective communication and proactive participation.

After the AI session, the co-facilitators made a presentation about it to BC's Assessment Committee. In their presentation, they used segments from the video, Celebrate What's Right with the World, which they also had used in the AI session. This helped the Committee get a better sense of what the session was like. The Committee then formulated plans for building on the AI pilot test.

There was a strong interest among the Committee and the BC president to use AI more broadly. The Parsons planned to continue working with the Assessment Committee and the president as they put plans in place to build on the experience.

The co-facilitators said, "Our main wish for the inquiry was that people would grasp the significance of the philosophy of AI."

Beverly Parson's 'personal best' was the involvement of two young Claremont University students of AI. They were involved in the planning, implementation and follow up activities, and reported that it was a tremendous learning experience for them. She also enjoyed hearing comments from participants, e.g., "I really feel if more staff would participate we would become a community working together again!"

## Houston Community College, Northwest Campus, TX

Maya Durnovo, Zach Hodges, Gilda McFail, Debbie Sharp and Connie Stone at Houston Community College - Northwest, co- facilitated the five generic processes of Appreciative Inquiry on the positive topic of Our Model of Excellence: Celebrating Our Best! beginning at a College Spring convocation. The Inquiry was facilitated over several sessions involving up to 100 faculty and staff, generating energy to continue the conversation in the Fall. According to President Hodges, in just half a day, faculty and staff members: (1) celebrated successes and had fun; (2) recognized excellence from the past and present that the College wanted to carry into the future; (3) discovered that positive questioning leads to positive change; and (4) reminded themselves of the "power of the question" so they could take this power into their classrooms and offices.

The Provocative Proposition the faculty and staff developed was, "Unwavering in our quest for excellence, we who work and learn at Northwest College: set high expectations for ourselves and each other; support each other's achievements; and make time to recognize and celebrate both individual and collective successes. Northwest College - a proud community."

They also created a Bumper Sticker: "Learning, Serving, Excelling: Northwest College - a proud community," and three Strategic Intentions: (1) Time will be set aside in convocations for sharing and celebrating individual and group successes, progress and accomplishments; (2) A place will be created on the Northwest College portal for the ongoing sharing of success stories; and (3) The Bumper Sticker version of the Provocative Proposition will be incorporated into a graphical element that can be included with all official College communication, similar to a logo or letterhead.

> "We were warned that people would leave after lunch - people stayed and were engaged."

According to Hodges, the "afterglow", i.e., what the team's best experiences were related to facilitating the Inquiry, were: "the passion with which Northwest administrators, faculty, and staff serve students; for most, teaching is a calling; strong belief in the community college mission of changing lives; the joy in the room as stories were shared; Everyone had a story to share; NW College Leadership modeled and continues to model appreciative behavior; and we were warned that people would leave after lunch - people stayed and were engaged."

## Southern State Community College, OH

> "Witnessing the enthusiasm for the College and colleagues' interest in being a part of the 'team" was priceless . . . The power of a positive attitude was readily apparent throughout this process."

Nicole Roades, director of institutional advancement at Southern State Community College in Ohio, facilitated an AI Summit on Creating a Culture That Embraces Learning: You Design It! at her College. Southern State was embarked upon becoming a learning college; the Inquiry was one initiative to move people forward.

Roades said, "Witnessing the enthusiasm for the College and colleagues' interest in being a part of the 'team' was priceless . . . The power of a positive attitude was readily apparent throughout this process."

The idea to host a workshop designed to address the Southern State culture was initiated during a Learning College Coordinating Committee meeting. This particular Committee, which Roades had been involved with since its inception, felt as though the initiatives it was bringing forth to the entire College community were being met with confused hesitation and in some cases, utter resistance. This forced the Committee to reevaluate its purpose. It was through this reevaluation that members opted to take a step backward and begin looking deeper into the College's culture for possible explanations to the challenges the Committee was facing. It was hoped that bringing different sectors of the College together for interactive conversation, they would, at minimum, be building teamwork, which would hopefully open minds to some of the Learning College initiatives.

The morning of the AI Summit (Ludema, et al), the College was met with inclement weather conditions and a delayed opening. In spite of this challenge, 49 people showed up for the session - 22 teaching staff and 27 non-teaching staff. The session began with a brief overview of its purpose, definitions of organizational culture and development of ground rules for the day.

Participants quickly moved into paired interviews, using the following Interview Guide.

100

1. Best Experience: Tell me a story about a time when you felt most alive, worthwhile and eager when learning. What made it a motivating and exciting experience - one in which you were glad to be involved? What were some of the behaviors that others exhibited that motivated and supported your learning? What did you do to motivate and support your learning?

2. Values: What are the things that you value about yourself, your work and Southern State?

Yourself: Without being humble, what do you value most about yourself - as a lifelong learner, human being, friend, parent, citizen, co-worker, and so on?

Your Work: When are you feeling best about your work, what do you value about it?

Southern State: What is it about Southern State that you value? What is the single most important thing that Southern State has contributed to your life?

3. Three Wishes: If you had three wishes for your work environment at Southern State what would they be?

4. Core Life-Giving Factor: What do you think is the core value or factor that allows Southern State to pull through during difficult times? If this core value/factor did not exist, how would that make Southern State totally different than it currently is?


Upon returning to the full group, each pair teamed up with other pairs to form groups of eight. From this point, the small groups discussed their interviews and developed a list of highlights that resulted from their conversations. These comprehensive lists were distilled into three to five themes.

The participants felt that the most important themes that needed to be included in creating a culture that embraced learning were: freedom; changing lives; positive attitude; supportive family-like atmosphere; and focus on students.

Once the key themes were identified, the groups moved toward ways of expressing those themes, first in visual images, then in word images or Provocative Propositions.

"Ideally," Roades said, "we would have synthesized all of the ideas into a single Proposition but because of limited time, we wrapped up the workshop focusing on just one, randomly selected Proposition. From this Proposition, the entire group was briefly challenged to begin contemplating actions or behaviors they could exhibit as a group and individually to support this desired culture.

"My . . . thoughts regarding this workshop reflect an overwhelming sense of positive collaboration and a desire to build on the forward-thinking and cooperative momentum. Participants left the room making comments like, 'This is the best thing we've ever done,' 'We need to do more of this,' and 'I had no idea they felt like we were part of the 'family'. Several people even commented that they felt as though the SSCC culture was already reflective of the themes identified in the workshop but they agreed there is always something more that could be done to further advance this desired culture.

"It could safely be concluded that the workshop was received well and was a step in the right direction toward learning more about our organizational culture and, ultimately, the type of culture that embraces learning. Although the Learning College Coordinating Committee has not reconvened since the workshop, as a result of this workshop, I suspect we will have a clearer understanding of the needs of our constituents and a better approach to introducing initiatives related to the Learning College."

Based on outcomes of the Summit, Roades made some recommendations to the College president: "To continue building on the positive results of the workshop, I offer you several recommendations. First, the issues that came up during the workshop, the Parking Lot issues, must be addressed. It would be a good idea for you to join the Learning College Committee when we devise the plan for addressing the issues and I can inform you of the next meeting date. Many of the issues were trivial but a few more sensitive issues were documented and require your guidance in addressing them. Second, the Learning College Committee needs to begin coordinating the 'next step.' Because we ran out of time for in-depth discussion regarding the design and implementation stage, I suggest we start where we left off and begin coordinating an activity to further address what we can do to create or sustain a culture that embraces learning. Lastly, because of the tremendous positive response of this workshop, I think it appropriate to continually seek opportunities to bring both teaching and non-teaching staff together on a more frequent basis."

*Student Engagement*

Southside Virginia Community College, VA

> **"I was thrilled when an advisor and a student voluntarily admitted that they had planned to leave early, but were so involved and fascinated by this approach, they decided to skip their other meetings and stay in this one. I knew then that AI was working."**

Stanley Johnson participated in a Virginia Community College System AIFT. He was an associate professor of English at Southside Virginia Community College and also a co-advisor to one of SVCC's two main campuses' Phi Theta Kappa International Honor Societies. PTK focuses on projects that serve PTK members, the College and the community. Four PTK officers, three co-advisors and an at-large member were selected to be both the Core Group and the Inquiry Group for an Appreciative Inquiry, a total of eight people. They identified PTK's "hot topics" as: lack of success in service projects and lack of participation by the membership.

Johnson helped the group re-frame the topics into High Energy Participation and Stronger Unity - what they wanted to create more of. The group then "tweaked" the generic Interview Guide to focus on the positive topics, then paired off and interviewed each other. While the group didn't collaboratively create a Provocative Proposition for the group as a whole, they did create Individual Dream Statements and Individual Commitments that they fulfilled.

Stanley's 'personal best' experience came after the group brainstormed the themes and put them on the wall as a scatter gram, more than an hour into the Inquiry. "I was thrilled when an advisor and a student voluntarily admitted that they had planned to leave early, but were so involved and fascinated by this approach, they decided to skip their other meetings and stay in this one. I knew then that AI was working." Stanley reported that, "Last Friday night, the Honor Society had its Valentine's Dance, and it was the first successful event we have sponsored in two years."

*Student Recruitment and Retention*

Edison Community College, OH

Sandra Brubaker was associate vice president for student development and enrollment management at Edison Community College in Ohio. Edison's staff consisted of 165 full and part-time permanent employees and several hundred adjunct faculty members. Enrollment at Edison had steadily grown over a period of six or seven years. Its post-

> **"I was truly amazed by how the process influenced the attitudes of the participants."**

secondary population -those students who were concurrently enrolled in high school and college - had nearly tripled the previous two years, primarily due to marketing of that program. However, although the traditional-age student enrollment had increased, the non-traditional population had decreased at an alarming rate. Hence, Edison was facing an overall four percent decline in enrollment in the fall.

The term, Strategic Enrollment Management (SEM), had a negative history at Edison. Approximately eight years earlier, Edison had held a forum that was inclusive of all staff during which they created many initiatives on a variety of predetermined topics. Many of these initiatives did not come to fruition. At the same time, a SEM committee was formed; it existed for almost five years, but lacked direction and purpose. Finally, it ceased to meet.

One of Brubaker's goals was to revitalize SEM. She was at a loss for how to do this until she participated in an AIFT. She said that she immediately knew that AI was a way to revitalize SEM.

After several meetings with her College president, they jointly determined that Edison needed to focus upon recruitment and retention, largely because of the projected enrollment trends. Also, Edison had no clear retention plan. After consulting with her new assistant dean of student development and enrollment management, Michael Perry, Brubaker began planning an Inquiry, an Open Forum. Untrained in AI, Perry was a bit skeptical about the "magic" that Brubaker believed the model could produce. Still, he did his best to learn about the theory, research and practice of AI on his own.

Prior to the Open Forum, Brubaker and Perry decided that they needed to involve students in the Inquiry, to find out why they were attracted to Edison and why they continued their education there. Over 100 students were interviewed in a two-week period. They used a variety of techniques to interview students. Some student interviews were conducted outside the classroom and some in the classroom. Several instructors allowed the facilitators to utilize some of their class time for interviews.

The facilitators provided a brief explanation of the interview process and purpose to the students. The students then paired up and took turns interviewing each other. They then came back to the large group where Brubaker and/or Perry facilitated a dialogue about the stories in which life-giving forces and common themes emerged. After the students identified common themes, Perry and Brubaker met and processed all of the stories and themes. These student-generated stories and themes were then presented to staff in a PowerPoint presentation at the Open Forum.

The Inquiry topic for the Open Forum was Students First! Attracting and Keeping Students at Edison . . . Success by Design. No mention was made of SEM. Staff members paired up to share their stories with one another before coming back to share the highlights of their partners' stories in small table-groups. The table-groups then brainstormed the life-giving forces from the stories, generating a list of 16 high-energy themes. Then each table-group selected the theme that was most important to them, i.e., what they most wanted to create more of. According to Brubaker, the groups had lots of fun creating and sharing visual images of their themes in songs, skits, interpretive dances, etc.

Then, based on their most important theme, each table-group developed a word image, or Provocative Proposition, of recruitment and retention at its best, and some Strategic Intentions, which they shared with the large group.

Individuals then made Individual Commitments, Offers or Requests to move forward the Intentions in which they personally were most interested. People moved around the room, self-organizing to form new conversation groups. Committees were then formed to further discuss some of the proposed initiatives. Overall, a dozen initiatives emerged.

According to Brubaker, "There was definitely an atmosphere of POSITIVENESS and appreciation for the 'time to talk.' I heard several people comment, 'We should do this every month.' Or 'We should do this several times a year!' 'This was a valuable experience.' 'I feel as though we looked at where we've been and where we can go.' Mainly, it gave people a renewed sense of energy and, perhaps more importantly, ownership in recruitment and retention initiatives. People were WILLING to participate on another committee!"

Brubaker said, "Since the Forum, I have had a number of faculty and staff members stop by my office to offer more ideas. I actually convinced a faculty member to serve on the resulting Students First! Steering Committee because of the ideas and dedication he shared after the Open Forum."

In terms of planned follow-up, Brubaker said, "Prior to the Open Forum, Michael and I met with our College president and presented a structure which would facilitate moving any resulting initiatives forward (even though we didn't know what they would be at the time). Michael agreed to chair the Students First! Steering Committee, which oversaw the initiatives generated in the Open Forum. Members of the Committee were selected from the project committees. Michael also began chairing the College's Grants Committee to seek external funding for these and other initiatives in support of recruitment and retention. The Steering Committee keeps track of initiatives and completion of the initiatives. Notices of achievements are posted College-wide and become part of the marketing efforts of the College."

Brubaker anticipated that a follow-up presentation/celebration would be held the following fall. She also thought it would be important for the president and President's Council members to acknowledge individual contributions and team efforts throughout the year.

Brubaker said she had "wished for a POSITIVE experience where the process would promote creativity and a positive atmosphere, resulting in some initiatives that people would become excited about! Given the history of SEM, as explained above, I was nervous about people coming to the session with the predisposed idea that it would be boring and useless. I think they were pleasantly surprised! I was truly amazed by how the process influenced the attitudes of the participants.

"I personally learned about the power of AI. The inquiry also gave me confidence that I understand the process and how it works, and that I can facilitate it effectively. I plan to offer a training session in using AI to our leadership group in Spring 2006. I also was reminded by more than one person about how we need to take the time to talk with one another more often. I was overjoyed (and appalled!) when someone suggested that we needed to do this 'once a month!'

"I thoroughly enjoyed watching Michael, my co-facilitator's face, when a participant stood up and proclaimed his love of Edison and people began clapping and hugging each other. He turned to me with disbelief and whispered, 'Well, I now proclaim you the Queen of Warm and Fuzzy.' And to think that he had been doubtful about the power of AI prior to the session!"

*Teaching and Learning*

Teaching for a Change Conference, CO

Mike McHargue, retired counselor at Foothill College in California, facilitated a three-hour Inquiry at the Teaching for a Change Conference in Colorado. Mike worked with 30 faculty and staff from 28 different institutions, mostly community colleges. The positive topic was Enhancing Student Learning Through Positive Instructional Change. The Inquiry focused on Appreciative Pedagogy (see Chapter Five for more on this topic).

McHargue said, "I was delighted at how well the Appreciative Inquiry adaptation worked. They loved the interviews (duh!) and apparently didn't find it too awkward to learn AI with a group they wouldn't follow up with. They seemed enthusiastic about completing their individual homework." Small groups worked through the processes of Discovery, Dream and Design. Their homework was to make an individual Commitment to initiate some positive practice during the first two weeks of the upcoming fall term.

## References for Chapter Eight

Celebrate What's Right With the World [DVD]. StarThrower.

Ludema, J., D. Whitney, B. Mohr & T. Griffin (2003). *The appreciative inquiry summit: a practitioner's guide for leading large-group change*. San Francisco: Berrett-Koehler.

Merrill, D. W. & R. H. Reid (1999). *Personal styles & effective performance*. Boca Raton: CRC Press.

The Power of Words (DVD). CRM Learning.

Stavros, J., D. Cooperrider & L. Kelley (2003). *Strategic inquiry > appreciative intent: inspiration to SOAR, a new framework for strategic planning*. London: AI Practitioner, November.

Watkins, J. M. & B. Mohr (2003). Appreciative inquiry for organization change: theory, practice and application. Unpublished workshop resource book.

# Chapter Nine

## EVERYDAY AI

### Changing the Conversation at the Water Cooler

Ralph Kelly, longtime AI practitioner, captured the essence of Appreciative Inquiry with his comment that AI is really about "changing the conversation at the water cooler" (Kelly, 2003), what the author thinks of as "everyday ai" – small lettered ai, not capped.

> "AI is about changing the conversation at the water cooler . . . filling the organization with positive stories of success. "

While some initiatives are designed for whole systems, large scale change, others can be as simple as asking a question that shifts the topic of conversation from one that has spiraled down to negativity – a fairly common occurrence known as the "woe is me" syndrome – to one of hope and possibilities. Here are a few examples of ways of changing the conversation.

### At Faculty Meetings

When a conversation has turned to negativity, ask a question that shifts the energy or reframes the conversation. An example: "It sounds like the administration (or X) is really making you angry or upset right now. What would it look like if the administration was behaving really well in this situation?" Listen for the answer or answers. Then ask a follow-up question: "Has there ever been a time when the administration behaved really well in this situation? If so, when was it? Who was involved? What did you do?" Then see if the group can talk about what they are learning from this example.

### At Administrative Meetings

> **Change the conversation, from problems to possibilities.**

When a conversation has turned to negativity, ask a question that shifts the energy or reframes the conversation. An example: "It sounds like the faculty (or X) is really making you angry or upset right now. What would it look like if the faculty was behaving really well in this situation?" Listen for the answer or answers. Then ask a follow-up question: "Has there ever been a time when the faculty behaved really well in this situation? If so, when was it? Who was involved? What did you do?" Then see if the group can talk about what they are learning from this example.

### At Santa Rosa Junior College, CA

Jennifer Mann, faculty member in the disabilities resource department at Santa Rosa Junior College in California, contributed these ideas for using an appreciative approach to everyday activities.
(1) Open each committee meeting with "What's working in your [job, life, productivity, creativity, etc.] right now?"
(2) Obtain feedback at every presentation by asking "What worked?" and "What would you like more of?"
(3) Have seasoned employees agree to be interviewed by new hires during a 30-60 minute Brown Bag lunch. Or have cross-components ask each other (i.e., classified ask administrators, etc.)

Sample questions:
What are the stories that have lasted over the years? Tell one.

What are our treasured artifacts? Where are they? Why are they treasures?

Who are the people we have to thank for our reputation? What else do we have to be thankful for?

What does this institution celebrate?

Where is the true pulse of the place?

How do people re-energize themselves? Maintain their passion?

What are the financially sustaining sources for the institution?

What have been the traumas and how were they resolved? What effects linger?

What is still needed here?

Give examples of the powerful people here and the influential people [by title]. What is the difference?

(4) During Accreditation Self Study, use the collegial interview process to get people talking about WHAT WORKS around the institution or district. Randomly pair up people in twos or threes to ask three simple questions. Sample structure:

a. BACKWARD - Recall a time when [there was success, pride, sense of accomplishment, etc.] in the institution. Tell the whole story.

b. INWARD - What does it mean to you to [be successful, proud, etc.]?

c. FORWARD - Imagine it is one year from now and the institution is a role model in the nation. How did it get to be that way? What were the practices and conditions that led us to that great recognition?

NOTE: Change any language inside the [ ] to suit your needs

(5) Facilitate a conversation between three units, such as student services and academic affairs or financial aid and admissions and records. Allow them to clarify their values, share their personal visions and then present a colleague whom they have interviewed using a variation of the three questions above.

(6) Use appreciative reflection prior to any conflict resolution conversation. Ask the parties to reflect on what <u>does</u> work or what they <u>do</u> appreciate about the perceived adversary. Ask them to prepare a list of what they would like more of in the relationship. Then get them to share those items and move toward agreements. It completely avoids the idea of delving into the drama of the past (See Chapter Six on Human Resource Development and Conflict Resolution).

(7) For any retreats or departmental community building activities, use AI to prepare the participants for interaction. Have them interview each other prior to arriving, then facilitate a report-out of what was discovered in the course of the interviews.

(8) For any large gathering, take 10 minutes to have everyone chat with their neighbors by asking three interview questions. Then ask 10 people to form a line and answer one of the questions into the microphone for the benefit of the entire room.

(9) Have participants in a large group write their brief answers on sticky notes, then place their notes on butcher paper posted at the exit door so everyone in the room participates in giving input to any topic. Compile the entire list for publication. Again, the structure is answering a positive inquiry.


*In The Classroom and Other Teaching and Learning Environments*

Here are a few more ideas for how to use an appreciative approach to teaching and learning that were developed by the author.

*For Teachers.* When reviewing assignments and assessments, circle or underline the ones that are correct (in green ink) rather than the ones that are incorrect (in red ink). Ask the student to reflect on the assignment or assessment and write a sentence about the strengths these "right answers" indicate about her or his current competencies.

*For Counselors.* When counseling students, ask them what they are best at, how they learn best, etc. Encourage them to build on their strengths.

*For Students.* When asked to give feedback about instructors, tell them what most worked for you in the teaching and learning process, not what didn't work. Be specific and concrete. Ask them to do more of it.

## Reenergizing An Inquiry: Strategic Learning Circles

Once a community college has been through several cycles of Inquiry – the five generic processes discussed in Chapter One – people may begin to lose some energy for what once held high energy. At that point, the community college leaders or consultants need to help the group find ways to reenergize the Inquiry. In addition to celebrating stories of success, The author suggested one process for doing that to Judy Walters when she was president at Berkeley City College (formerly Vista College) that Judy used at a two-hour session, following months of extensive Strategic Planning.

Stetson said, "The Appreciative Inquiry community is beginning to call this process 'Strategic Learning' as contrasted to 'Strategic Planning,' which makes it clear that it is an ongoing process (not resulting in a "plan" per se, but in ongoing organizational learning). That fits nicely with Senge's notion of a Learning Organization. So you could call these sessions Strategic Learning Circles".

Put all of the provocative propositions, strategic intentions and individual commitments in a document/handout and distribute widely in advance of the session. Ask people to sit in a circle (or circles, if the group is too large for one circle) and share any and all success stories - with a focus on impact and/or results and/or outcomes, either relating to Vista College as a whole (organizational learning), to a particular group/department (departmental learning) and/or to students (student learning). Remember, as AI practitioner Ralph Kelly (2003) said, "AI is about changing the conversations at the water cooler . . . filling the organization with positive stories of success." Everyone will have some sort of story of success, whether or not it relates to (an already past history!) provocative proposition, strategic intention, or individual commitment.

Then, after all of the stories are shared, have everyone take a minute or two to complete a Summary Sheet and submit it to you for compilation into a report, as well as for use in your newsletter.

## Summary Sheet

1. What was the most appreciative quotable quote that you heard?
2. What was the most compelling story that you heard?
3. What was the most "life-giving" moment for you as a listener?
4. Did you hear a particularly creative and/or innovative example of success? If so, describe it and what you learned from it.
5. Reflecting on all the stories you heard, what three themes stood out for you most?

After the Summary Sheets are completed, ask people to reflect on how they might learn from the success stories they've heard to create even more successes! In other words, ask them to look for 'best practices' among all the success stories that they can 'copy' and replicate. Record any responses on flip chart paper. The 'AI 5' (at Berkeley City College) can turn these responses into another Provocative Proposition. And the beat goes on . . .

Another way to do the reporting out of 'success stories' is to have people do an activity to demonstrate the success (skit, poem, song, etc.); in other words, not left brain, but right brain. Or create a 'Wall of Wonder' where everyone posts their drawings and you leave them up in the hallways. That way, people won't get burned out on words. Anything you and others can do to fill your college with positive stories and images all of the time will lead to positive actions. Positive image = positive action.

---

## Community Colleges and Appreciative Inquiry

Community colleges face an unknown future, one that seems to promise continuous deep, rapid and often turbulent change. To thrive in this environment, community colleges can create organizational cultures that help people thrive – environments that nourish ongoing creativity and innovation – for students, employees, communities and society at large. As these many stories of positive change attest, one promising way for community colleges to do this is through Appreciative Inquiry, a powerful approach to organizational change and development. Community colleges and our society need all the help – and hope – they can get.

# References for Chapter Nine

Cooperrider, D. L. & D. Whitney. (2005). *Appreciative inquiry: A positive revolution in change*. San Francisco: Berrett-Koehler.

Kelly, R. (2003). Oral comment made during an Appreciative Inquiry foundations workshop, co-facilitated by J. M. Watkins. Ben Lomond, CA. January.

# THE AUTHOR'S STORY

I was born on the beach (well, not literally, but close) in 1936 in Kitty Hawk, North Carolina - famous for being the site of the first powered flight. I had a near idyllic early childhood, if you don't count the time I almost drowned in the Atlantic. Saved by my older brother, Murray, I also had an older sister Saragay - now deceased - and a trusting mother Nannie who gave us the freedom to explore the Outer Banks on our own - the beach, the ocean, the legendary sand dunes (which, according to my brother, are no longer there), and the Albemarle and Currituck Sounds - nature at her very, very best.

After briefly attending first grade (no kindergarten in Kitty Hawk), Nannie and my siblings headed for the "land of opportunity" - the mythic "up North" where I went to public schools in Elizabeth and Union, New Jersey, graduating from Union High in 1954. After working for a year to earn money and to make up a few prep courses that I needed for college, I was unaccountably accepted by Swarthmore College, which I attended for only a year and a half before leaving to marry. My early childhood and my brief time at Swarthmore were both valuable gifts.

Thirteen years later, I became a single mom to my two daughters, Laurel and Nancy Lee - two more valuable gifts. Then, while working full time at two different community colleges, I earned an associate degree in liberal arts from Wenatchee Valley College, a bachelor's degree in writing and development from The Evergreen State College, a master's degree in individualized studies/organizational behavior from Central Washington University and a doctor's degree in higher education from Nova Southeastern University.

In 1971, I began my 26-year community college career at Wenatchee Valley (Community) College, retiring from the (Community) College of Marin in 1997. At Wenatchee, my fifth gift was James R. Davis, president, who was the best "people developer" I have ever worked for or with. My administrative assignments in those two community colleges included vice president for planning and development, interim vice president for student and special services, dean for development and information services, director of public affairs and development, assistant to the president/director of community and institutional development, interim campus dean, director of information and development, and public information officer. My faculty assignments included: English, management and supervision, business, mass media, public relations, communications, journalism and newspaper production. I also served on the Academic Senate and chaired the curriculum committee.

Along the way, I taught part-time at many two and four-year public colleges and universities. Currently I am a faculty mentor and assessor in Walden University's Ph.D. in Education program, specializing in Community College Leadership. I also serve as an executive coach to community college leaders and as an educational advisor to Distance EDU Learning's revolutionary online learning management software called Fintelo.

In 1979, I began consulting part time to community colleges and, in 1989, founded and served as president of a consulting firm, Company of Experts.net, until 2005. As a consultant, I served more than 125 different organizations, mostly community colleges, in: organization development, including Appreciative Inquiry; board development; administrative development; faculty development; and staff development.

My professional articles and monographs have been published in: *Leadership Abstracts*, League for Innovation in the Community College; *Consulting Today*; *Appreciative Inquiry in the Community College: Early Stories of Success*, League for Innovation in the Community College; *Network*, National Council for Staff, Program, and Organizational Development; *Academic Leadership*, Chair Academy; *Community College Times*, American Association of Community Colleges; *Cooperative Learning and College Teaching*, an international newsletter of New Forums Press, Inc.; *FACCCTS*, the journal of the Faculty Association of California Community Colleges; *Community College Journal*; *Network*, Association of California Community College Administrators; *New Directions for Teaching and Learning*, Jossey-Bass; *Accreditation Notes*, Accrediting Commission for Community & Junior Colleges, Western Association of Schools and Colleges; *NORCAL Community College Research Group*, a Northern California newspaper; *The News*, California Association of Community Colleges; *Management Report*, Association of California Community College Administrators; *Proceedings of the First National Conference on Classroom Research*, University of California at Berkeley; *Community Services Catalyst*; and *Small Town*.

Awards I most cherish are: The Lorraine Barry Individual Leadership Award from the California Community College Council for Staff and Organizational Development, named in honor of my late friend and colleague at College of Marin; with Charles R. Miller, Western Region John Fry Individual Merit Award from the National Council for Staff, Program, and Organizational Development for outstanding contributions to staff, program, and organizational development at the regional and local level; National Leadership Award from the National Council for Staff, Program, and Organizational Development for outstanding contributions in writing, research and advocacy that promoted the goals of staff, program, and organizational development at the national level; Practitioner's Hall of Fame by Nova Southeastern University for excellent contributions leading to the improvement of educational practice; and a Rising Star award by League for Innovation in the Community College.

Regarding the Rising Star, I probably didn't "rise" as high as the League thought I might, i.e., to become a community college president. Rather, when that became a possibility, I broke free of organizational life - at heart an Outer Banks kid needing freedom.

When I was in my sixties, my sixth gift was living again, for seven years, right on the beach (well, not literally, but close) in Dillon Beach, California - a beach community that is remarkably similar to the Outer Banks of my youth. I think of these two great oceans as having held me and my life in place, sort of like bookends.

I consider Fintelo and this book to be my final contributions to the community college world, a world I dearly love. My hope is that both products will live longer than I do and will be both inspiring and useful to community colleges. While I don't expect to be spirited away anytime soon - Nannie is now 93, so I have pretty fair genes - I'm ready to move on to other things.

I am very grateful for the full and rich life I have been privileged to live so far. And I'm looking forward to the surprise of my seventh gift.

Nancy E. Stetson, Ed.D.
Rohnert Park, Northern California
*November 2007*

112